New Developments in

ECONOMICS

and

BUSINESS
EDUCATION

New Developments in

ECONOMICS

and

BUSINESS EDUCATION

Edited by David Whitehead and David Dyer

KOGAN PAGE

Published in association with the Institute of Education,
University of London

First published in 1991

Kogan Page Limited
120 Pentonville Road
London N1 9JN

© Institute of Education, University of London, 1991

British Library Cataloguing in Publication Data
A CIP record for this book is available from the British Library.
ISBN 07494 0340 3

Typeset by BookEns Ltd, Baldock, Herts.
Printed and bound in Great Britain by Biddles Ltd, Guildford

Contents

Notes on Contributors

Alain Anderton is a part-time teacher, Codsall High School, and author.

Steven Blowers is Adviser in Business Education, East Sussex.

David Butler is Adviser for Economic and Business Education, Kent County Council.

Ian Chambers is Adviser in Business Education for Tameside.

Anna Craft is Lecturer in Primary Education, Open University.

David Dyer (co-editor) is Lecturer in Business Education, Institute of Education, University of London, and Director, Cambridge Business Studies Project.

Steve Hodkinson is Senior Lecturer in Education, University of Manchester.

David Lines is Lecturer in Business Education, Institute of Education, University of London, and Assistant Director, Cambridge Business Studies Project.

Maureen Maurice is Head of Business Studies, Walton Comprehensive School, Peterborough.

Ian Pearce is Operations Director for the School Curriculum Industry Partnership, University of Warwick.

Marjorie Pirie is Head of Business Studies, Jack Hunt School, Peterborough.

Linda Thomas is Senior Lecturer in Education (Economics), Institute of Education, University of London.

Nancy Wall is Head of Economics, Beacon Community School, Crowborough.

William Walstad is Professor of Economics and Director of the National Center for Research in Economic Education, University of Nebrasksa, Lincoln.

David Whitehead (co-editor) is Senior Lecturer in Economics Education, Institute of Education, University of London.

Preface

The 1988 Education Reform Act (ERA) gave rise to the most radical reform of education since the 1944 Act. The ERA included the commitment to review the situation with the passage of time and in the light of experience, and to amend the law if necessary.

In the wake of the Act, as many schools approached forward curricular planning on a narrow front, teachers of economics and business studies were concerned about the future place of their subject in the curriculum. Morale among most of them was not high. However, the first amendments to the law (announced by the Secretary of State for Education and Science in his North of England speech in January, 1991) provide more scope than was hitherto envisaged for the development of specialist courses in economics and business studies for pupils aged 14–16 within the National Curriculum framework.

Teachers in these subject fields can therefore approach the future with greater self-confidence and with the knowledge that subjects like economics and business studies are recognized as being important for the personal, social, academic and vocational development of pupils and students.

The publication of this book is therefore timely, and is intended to be of help to all those concerned with the teaching of economics and business studies in a situation which has continuing scope for development and innovation.

Alan Walmsley, OBE
formerly HM Inspector of Schools

1 Introduction

David Whitehead and David Dyer

Company accountants, and those for whom they prepare a balance sheet, know that while it is only a snapshot of a rapidly changing scene, it should represent a true and fair view of the position as it is seen within one set of conventions. In this book we have similar problems, except that we are able to present a diversity of views on the rapidly changing fields of business and economics education.

Nancy Wall begins her chapter on 'The 16–19 Economics Curriculum': 'Now and over the next few years, the 16–19 curriculum is and will be the subject of intense debate.' Herein lies the impetus for this book. The choices that face teachers in both Economics and Business Studies are bewildering and daunting; the claims made for various courses and syllabuses are confusing. But the problems are not confined to the 16 to 19 age group nor to the content of teaching. An equally challenging debate is taking place on pre-16 education, and on the nature and purposes of assessment.

We do not present these articles as a 'crystal ball' which will accurately predict the future or provide a simple instrument for decision making. We aim to present the major issues in a single compendium, to illuminate and interpret the present position and to report why we have reached it and the potential for development.

In Chapters 2 to 7, the focus is on developments in Economics education; on ways in which the curriculum does and might reflect the wider vision now embedded in the National Curriculum up to age 16 and which is increasingly influencing courses of study and modes of assessment post-16. In this context, we are offered a positive and helpful insight into the perspective and impact of 'Economics Education for All'.

Business Studies presents a different but linked field of study, in which most of the issues raised for Economics education are relevant. Those who have been teaching the subject for GCSE face a future for which there is still no clear frame of reference and no defined opportunities either within or outside the National Curriculum. Other teachers face the challenge of teaching Business Studies within 'Technology' without the experience which would support their efforts.

Economics has evolved a more concrete and generally agreed concept of its nature, and the debate is about how flexibility and creative and insightful scope for development can be maintained. In Business Studies, the debate has not progressed so far, and concerns its actual nature and scope. What should be offered as the essential core of the subject; how should it be presented to students; what is its relationship with the wide range of other disciplines upon which it draws; how should it be assessed?

Despite these differences of focus, there is much in Sections 1 and 2 of concern and interest to us all. Ideas relating to teaching across the curriculum; to the advantages and difficulties of modular courses; to ways in which the two subjects might be pursued in an integrated fashion; to methods of assessment. These are just a few of the matters of common professional approach.

Modular courses, in particular, offer new opportunities to those wishing to teach both Economics and Business Studies or to combine the challenges which each presents, within an integrated course. In this respect, the 'Wessex Project' post-16 and GCSE courses such as those of Redbridge and Tameside are good exemplars.

The Wessex Project may well provide a glimpse of the future for those who see post-16 courses as being more broadly based. It presents a common core approach in year one, and then a choice of specialization in either Business or Economic Studies in year two. The base is further broadened by the provision of elective modules which present the subjects in a much wider context. It opens up an old but nonetheless vigorous debate between those who favour the 'broad canvas' and those who advocate the 'thorough rigorous understanding' approach.

We hope that the 'dynamic' of the present position is made clear. Nothing is written on tablets of stone, and some of the ideas may not stand the test of time (or the market!). Virtually all the developments discussed in this publication are in the initial and volatile stages of an uncertain product life cycle; all are subject to continuing change. The other important common feature is that they are all teacher-led and/or require a degree of teacher participation, which could be regarded as a burden but should be viewed as an opportunity.

Our objectives in presenting perceptions of the changes which are taking place are, on the one hand, to provide an informative but challenging set of views which will help to define the present position, and on the other, to convey a sense of the exciting developments in which we may all participate, the direction and nature of which can be influenced by those who teach. Such influence may be exerted directly through participation in courses and assessment procedures as they develop, or indirectly through the course choices that are made. We wish to encourage and enable a pro-active rather than a reactive response to change.

In pursuit of these objectives, we have sought contributions from writers among the foremost in their field, who have been positive contributors to the developments about which they write. Their views are not necessarily those of the editors, and they are not universally consistent one with the other. The deliberate debate embodied within the approaches taken as a whole is one which we hope will continue among readers. It might well contribute to the changes which are ahead.

In Section 3 we offer support to the teacher attempting to pick a path through the massive and bewildering jungle of resource materials and contacts. The approach is comprehensive, but it is not meant to be exhaustive. We have tried to avoid the danger of presenting so much that it is unhelpful, whilst meeting the need to provide for a wide range of different courses in individually effective ways. On this, and on all elements of the book, we would welcome your comments and suggestions, which may well become a contribution to a later edition.

To work with colleagues making current, cogent and challenging contributions to the curriculum and assessment in Business Studies and Economics is a privilege as well as a delight. Our thanks to them all.

SECTION 1:
ECONOMICS EDUCATION

2 The 16–19 Economics Curriculum: A Guide to Current and Likely Changes to the A Level and A/S Level Curriculum

Nancy Wall

Introduction

Now and over the next few years, the 16–19 curriculum is and will be the subject of intense debate. We need to take account of the changes wrought by GCSE and the National Curriculum. All syllabuses will be required to make adjustments, and some will change markedly.

One is faced with a choice between documenting a few boring certainties or taking the information available and making some assumptions about what will happen. The latter is more interesting but highly likely to be at least partly wrong when hindsight is possible.

Certain changes have taken place already. This chapter describes the two most innovative schemes currently operating, the Wessex and the Ridgeway Projects, and the framework which is being created by the National Curriculum Council (NCC), and the School Examination and Assessment Council (SEAC), within which further reforms will take place. We can only speculate as to what A level syllabuses will look like in 1994; nevertheless, such speculation is worthwhile, for it prepares us for the implementation of changes in which we will have a part.

Changes over the past five years: A-level examinations

The common core syllabus, published in 1983, was designed to give some degree of comparability to the various examination-board syllabuses. It outlined the established content of a traditional introductory course in such general terms, however, that its impact was minimal. Thus we have had a long period of stability (or is it stultification?) in A level Economics education. All that happened on the formal level between the mid-1970s and the late-1980s was that data response questions were slowly taken up by one board after another, Oxford being the last in 1985.

But this stable situation itself prompted numerous attempts at reform. Teachers are acutely aware of how overloaded syllabuses have become. In effect we have been under pressure to teach most of the traditional content, plus current controversies and their relevance to recent events. A consequence of this overloading is that too many students emerge with pass grades based on a quite limited understanding of the subject, and not a few misapprehensions.

This said, examination boards must be given credit for genuine attempts to innovate within the traditional framework. JMB and London have joined the Oxford and Cambridge board in extending their questions to include developing countries. All boards have moved to make more of their essay questions require the application of theory, although there are still major variations between them in this respect.

Three boards (London, AEB, and Cambridge) have set in motion new syllabuses. AEB began the process with a determined attempt to specify the syllabus more clearly. It responded to user pressure by elaborating something of what would, and would not, be required. Indifference curves and revealed preference are no longer required by any of these three. The revised Cambridge syllabus, to be examined first in 1992, additionally reduces the scope of traditional theory of the firm somewhat and introduces economic development, and for 1992 and 1993, a special subject, the Economics of the EC. Meantime, London has a draft syllabus upon which it is consulting interested teachers. This proposes some quite radical changes, with reduced emphasis on the theory of the firm, on the theory of marginal productivity, national income accounting, the components of aggregate demand and the minutiae of the monetary system. Increasing emphasis is proposed for market failure, welfare issues, current policy issues and economic development. There has been a very varied response to the proposals and at the time of writing no decisions have yet been taken.

These developments are in part a response to a debate over the last few years which has been fostered by the Economics Association. A number of articles have appeared in *Economics*, notably by Rosalind Levacic, exploring the needs of the future and analysing the positive and negative aspects of the present arrangements (see, for instance, Gavin et al., 1989; Levacic, 1987; McFarlane, 1988; Wall, 1986). Nevertheless, it remains the case that in general, although the examination system has done much to encourage good practice through the increasing emphasis on data response, and through extension of question coverage, the basic syllabus structure has remained unchanged for many years. Many teachers want to adopt innovative classroom strategies. But it is difficult to do so with an overloaded syllabus and traditional assessment procedures.

A/S levels

The rationale for A/S levels was to broaden students' studies into contrasting and complementary fields without loss of rigour. While it is apparent that the take-up of A/S courses has been disappointing nationally, they have nevertheless provided a degree of innovation. The London A/S incorporates an investigative study. Three of the four syllabuses involve a core and options structure. The potential exists, but given the very small number of students currently studying A/S level Economics, its impact is so far very limited (Livesey, 1987).

Resources

Partly under the influence of GCSE experience, many teachers have come to see themselves as classroom managers. They seek to provide a wide range of experiences for their students, with the emphasis on active learning. Well-taught, Economics has always involved student-centred learning activities. Traditional approaches include case studies, data analysis, theoretical exercises, comprehension exercises and industrial visits. Recent years have seen a major improvement in the range of resources available, including a good range of computer-based simulations. Computer databases are essential. In small groups, students can explore the data, seeking evidence (or the lack of it) for the theories they have encountered.

Very importantly, publishers have moved away from total reliance on staple texts and exercises directly related to practice for examination purposes. The *Economic Review* has made much useful material available. Two other major contributions are Paisley and Quillfeldt (1989) and *Discovering Economics* (Grey, 1989, 1990). The former presents a range of data on each topic, including tables, graphs and newspaper articles. It includes a wide range of questions, easy at first but very challenging later, on data analysis and on the application of economic theory. *Discovering Economics* is presented as a set of hypothesis-testing exercises. Relevant data is presented, with each hypothesis broken down into a set of necessary tasks. Questions are asked on the data; most importantly, the student is invited to evaluate the evidence and present a considered personal view. Both of these books must be used carefully, for they are sufficiently subtle and rigorous in their approach to confuse an inadequately prepared student. Used with care, they have immense value. They will, however, need frequent updating.

Beyond this, many teachers have sought to apply their pre-A level experience in fruitful ways. Brainstorming, debate, investigations, decision-taking exercises, group work and presentations, all have valuable parts to play in the A level experience. These are highly positive developments. Unfortunately, the heavily loaded syllabus hampers the innovative teacher. It takes some skill and experience to use these sometimes time-consuming approaches, *and* prepare students for a very demanding terminal examination. Perhaps more serious still, many teachers still prefer to use familiar strategies. The consequences are twofold:

we are not always capitalising on the gains from GCSE, and we are making the transition from GCSE to A level highly problematic for the student.

In this situation it is fortunate that the momentum for change is gathering pace. It is still more fortunate that a number of hardworking teachers have already begun the process of innovation.

The Ridgeway Project

The Ridgeway School in Wiltshire has a relatively small Sixth form. It saw A/S levels as highly desirable. But running new courses with no extra resources is difficult in a small Sixth Form where group sizes are often small. Ridgeway therefore set up its own modular A/AS scheme in collaboration with ULSEB. A level students take six modules, A/S, three. The Project covers seven subjects and enables them to co-teach (i.e., teach simultaneously) both A and A/S candidates. The project began in 1987, the first year of A/S teaching. At the time of writing (Summer 1990), the initial pilot project is much expanded and is shifting from Mode 3 to Mode 2. This means that Ridgeway School's initiators are no longer in control of the project; ULSEB now play a much larger part and so control both content and assessment procedures.

The foundation of the Economics syllabus is the core module, which includes opportunity cost, price theory, an elementary circular flow model and fiscal policy. This occupies the first term and is very much an introduction. The other five modules cover resource allocation; welfare economics and government; money inflation and unemployment; business in theory and practice; and an industrial study. Together the six modules cover the A level common core. An A/S course takes in the core module, plus two others. The content therefore differs little from a traditional A level. Remarkably, the project has achieved substantial innovation within this framework.

Though the initial objective of the Ridgeway project was to accommodate A/S courses, few students have actually opted for A/S Economics. The benefits of the project have turned out to lie elsewhere, in bringing about a complete change in the way students approach their studies. The initial assessment takes place at the end of the second module, after twenty weeks' teaching. This has a powerful effect on students' motivation. Furthermore, the emphasis in the classroom is upon investigation and presentation, and this has a very beneficial effect on students' confidence. Personal skills are further enhanced if they undertake the Industry study. The significance of this is that the students must address a real problem which currently faces a local firm. They must analyse the problem, using the economic techniques, theories and principles they have learned. In presenting solutions they must communicate effectively with the firm, and convince the teacher that they have examined the problem as an economist would. This greatly enhances the quality of students' skills, both in analysis and application, and in communication.

Coursework accounts for a further 50 per cent of assessment of the welfare economics module, in which students must make a case study in the field of education, health or housing. Thus the innovation lies in assessment procedures, and in learning styles. The approach builds upon GCSE; and it facilitates learning for those students who traditionally would have finished their education with O levels (the 'new' A level students), who are now increasing in number.

The Wessex Project

This is a much larger project covering a number of schools and colleges in Avon, Dorset, Gloucestershire, Somerset and Wiltshire, in collaboration with AEB. Teaching began in 1989. The objective of the project is 'to bridge the academic–vocational divide without loss of rigour or coherence'. To this end it uses active learning and student-centred approaches, records of achievement, and a modular structure. It is the most innovative development yet underway. It allows students to choose some of their modules, one of which may be from another relevant subject area. Also, some modules are inter-disciplinary in approach. So broadening of experience is possible. Further innovation is to be found in its linking of Economics with Business Studies.

In all subjects, an A level consists of a core (60 per cent) and four modules (40 per cent each). A/S levels similarly comprise a core and two modules. The cores provide continuity and are externally assessed. The modules provide choice and are assessed by coursework. The unique approach to Economics and Business Studies consists of a common core in the first year. In the second year, students choose between an Economics core and a Business Studies core, and proceed to an A level in one subject or the other (this is known as the Y-front model).

The common core consists of four elements: foundation, income, wealth and expenditure; people, markets and power; and change – the impact of change on business and the economy. The Economics core in the second year covers much of the A level common core which does not already appear in the first year core, ie the standard A level syllabus. It is therefore heavily loaded, reflecting the requirements of the examination board and of SEAC.

The available modules for Economics and Business Studies at present consist of a new business proposal; multi-national companies; the economic/business system of another country; cost-benefit analysis; law and the environment; development economics; accounting for business, and a local industry study. The modules are taught by means of supported self-study packages with strong emphasis on investigation and presentation.

An important feature of the project is that teachers devise their own strategies in collaboration with each other, giving mutual support. (In this as in other ways the Wessex Project has drawn inspiration from the Geography 16-19 Project). Strong links are developing with local firms. For participating teachers, there is considerable flexibility. If they so wish, they can teach the core in both years in quite traditional ways. However, a number of schools have chosen to teach both core and modules in innovative ways. The aims of the modules are to enhance study, investigative and research skills; and 'to create an awareness of the applications and implications of Economics in the world around us'. Students might investigate the impact of change by interviewing employees of a local firm, which has repeatedly made redundant then re-employed local residents as its sales have fluctuated. In general, a wide variety of resources can be provided to facilitate investigation; nevertheless, students have identified the availability of information as one of the main problems they have to face.

The typical pattern of student experience might follow a sequence of being introduced to relevant material and other teacher inputs; several small group tutorials; outside visits; investigation in libraries, newspapers, etc; reporting their findings and presenting them to the class. Thus the teacher provides lead lessons, resources and tutorial help.

Assessment criteria follow a broad pattern, covering seeking information; manipulating and evaluating material; and presentation. Fifty per cent of assessment will be by terminal examination, including a case study with four weeks preparation time built in. The other paper will consist of an unseen case study and questions based on stimulus and data response material. The modules are assessed by coursework. The remaining 10 per cent of assessment is based on teacher assessment of decision-making and application skills, communication and group work. The latter is especially important in that the focus is upon 'skills and processes which arise naturally as part of normal student classroom activity'.

In effect, the Wessex project has introduced innovations which foreshadow the likely changes to come through SEAC, perhaps going well beyond. It is possible to teach the entire course through the medium of case studies. The link with Business Studies may enhance the subject's apparent relevance to the real world. The emphasis on change and the dynamic aspects of the economy is in contrast to the predominantly static approach of traditional theory. The student-centred approach can be expected to give much help to the bewildered 'new' A level student.

In themselves the Wessex innovations are not as radical as they may seem. Good teachers have been using these strategies for years. The important change lies in moving to a mode of assessment which is sympathetic, rather than otherwise, to an investigative and student-centred approach. Some loss of Economics content should be expected, given the initial common core with Business Studies. Against this, the core skills identified by the National Curriculum Council are directly addressed and much enhanced by the Wessex approach.

As with the Ridgeway project, the teachers who are setting up the Wessex project are unsung heroes who deserve much credit. The experimental nature of the project is very much apparent. The insistence upon encouraging flexibility creates great possibilities, and also great responsibilities. A possible problem with modular courses is that they may lack coherence within the subject area. The possibility should be kept in mind in the process of course construction.

The impact of GCSE on 16-19 courses

Shortly before teaching for GCSE courses began in 1986, there were attempts at inservice training which drew large numbers of teachers into the process of curriculum reform. Even before this, from 1983 onwards, TVEI programmes required teachers to extend and develop their use of experiential learning strategies. Many Economics teachers were involved in these developments. Others helped to set up Economics awareness programmes.

It soon became clear that Economics teachers should use these experiences to enrich and develop their A level work. The framework within which they do so is much constrained, however, by the general examination structure.

The framework for change

We have seen that until now, change at A level has come piecemeal from a variety of sources. New kinds of resources and publications have influenced classroom strategies and tactics. Increasing use of data response for assessment has led to much improved skills in the handling and interpretation of data.

Some adjustments have been made to syllabuses. Now, change will accelerate. In 1994, the first Sixth Formers to have completed National Curriculum Key Stage 4 will begin their A level studies. By that time, all A and A/S syllabuses and their assessment schemes will have been resubmitted to SEAC for approval. SEAC will have compared each examination board's syllabus offering with the general principles laid down in 1991.

Though there is much talk of rationalization, which might reduce the total number of syllabuses, the present number for Economics (11 for A level, 5 for A/S) is not excessive, given the large number of candidates for Economics courses. It may be that there will be little or no reduction in the number of courses. Importantly, A level Economics is now the third most popular A level. Although the growth in numbers of candidates has been slower recently than that of Business Studies, A level Economics does not seem to be threatened by falling rolls.

SEAC's role

SEAC continues to relate to examination boards by voluntary agreement. Through the process of first approving, and then scrutinising A and A/S examinations at regular intervals, it seeks to influence. The general principles lay down guidelines showing examination boards what is required. They are likely to have an impact on practice throughout the system. However, SEAC's work can go beyond this since it can offer guidance to schools and colleges. This guidance is likely to cover ways in which courses can bring breadth and depth to individuals' studies, and prepare them for work and for further study.

The general principles

These guidelines, published in early 1991, are intended to give SEAC control over standards and over syllabus development. They may make for a smoother progression from GCSE to A level studies. They should create a clearer relationship between A and A/S courses. They are expected to find ways of making A level studies accessible to a wider range of students, perhaps through the use of records of achievement. These would give some credit for the progress made by weaker candidates.

SEAC will specify minimum and maximum weightings for coursework. There may be a change of emphasis in the skills being taught. Essay questions may count for a smaller proportion of the marks available. Data response and problem-solving questions may play an increasing part in assessment. There may eventually be provision for the use of credit transfers, which will integrate A level courses more closely with vocational courses. The general principles will give guidelines as to how core skills are to be built into A level study.

Integrating the core skills

The NCC statement of March 1990 specifies the core skills to be incorporated in A level. All A and A/S courses are to develop communication, problem solving and personal skills. In appropriate subjects, numeracy, IT skills and a modern language are to be incorporated. A and A/S Economics will be seen as appropriate vehicles for all the core skills except perhaps the modern language. Even there, some students may well be able to pursue an option which allows them to enhance their language skills, for example by undertaking coursework on the economy of a country whose language they are keen to study. It would seem that Economics is a subject which is ideally suited to the delivery of the core skills.

There is much work to be done on the means by which core skills will be embedded in A and A/S courses. However, in a purely speculative way, it is possible to envisage how the process could work. Written communication can be fostered by the use of a wider range of formats: report writing may be a feature of coursework. Oral communication may be enhanced in the researching of coursework and by teamwork on decision-taking exercises. Problem solving is already a feature of some types of questions used by Economics teachers. Will the firm's problems be solved by a price increase? Could import controls reduce unemployment? These are examples of questions which, if much developed and carefully specified, would lend themselves to a problem-solving approach. Personal skills can be developed through teamwork and through independent research. Information technology skills are fostered by the use of data bases which can be used to inform a wide range of issues already studied within A level Economics. Numeracy too is already enhanced by data work and could be developed further in similar ways.

The unknowns

While it seems certain that we shall develop leaner syllabuses, with some topics currently taught taking up much less time, the precise content is uncertain. Traditional theory of the firm seems likely to be downgraded (as AEB has already decided). Development Economics may be included and a determined effort to make courses less insular can be expected.

One possible response to the desire of all teachers to retain their favourite topics would be courses with a core and option module structure. These are already in use in A/S, and the Wessex and Ridgeway projects. This approach would facilitate the introduction of coursework.

What are the implications of widening access? Many people are concerned about the inappropriateness of current courses for the weaker candidate. The result may be much improved provision for them, giving credit for what they have achieved instead of N or U grades.

Will there be more combination courses? It is expected that combinations of humanities will be available soon at GCSE. Combined A level studies may provide a valued means of broadening experience. Cambridge already offer Economic and Political Studies, a popular course in some centres.

Will there be a midpoint examination? There is a felt need for an examination which goes beyond GCSE but is suitable for candidates for whom A level studies are too demanding. A/S courses could be used in this way, if adapted somewhat. It is not clear how the authorities view this possibility.

At the time of writing there are many uncertainties; it should be remembered though that existing innovations are providing valuable precedents which may well become the basis for more general adoption.

Acknowledgement

I am grateful for Alun Evans' help in preparing the section on the Ridgeway Project, and to Chris Vidler for help in researching the section on the Wessex Project.

References

Gavin, M, Shellard, M, and Swann, P (1989) ' "A" level Economics; the case for controversy', *Economics*. 25, No 106, pp 50-55.
Grey, D (ed.) (1989, 1990) *Discovering Economics, Macroeconomics, Microeconomics*. Causeway Press, Ormskirk.
Levacic, R (1987) 'What changes should be made to the "A" level Economics syllabus for the 1990s?, *Economics* 24, No 100, pp 97-105.
Livesey, F (1987) ' "A/S" level in Economics', *Economics* 23, No 99, pp 63-65.
McFarlane, W (1988) 'What changes should be made to the "A" level syllabus? A response to Rosalind Levacic', *Economics* 24, No 102, p 69.
Paisley, R and Quillfeldt, J (1989) *Economics Investigated*. Collins, London.
Wall, N (1986) 'Drawing a line: what are the limits at "A" level?, *Economics* 22, No 95. pp 105-7.

3 GCSE Economics

Alain Anderton

Introduction

In 1983, Sir Keith Joseph announced that O levels and CSEs would be replaced by a single system of examining at 16-plus. The General Certificate of Secondary Education (GCSE), first taken by candidates in summer 1988, has a number of distinctive features. All syllabuses offered for examination have to conform to a set of General National Criteria. Twenty-two subjects, ranging from Biology to Home Economics to Welsh literature, have their own subject-specific National Criteria. National Criteria lay down aims, assessment objectives, content, techniques of assessment and grade descriptions.

GCSE examinations should enable candidates to show that they 'know, understand and can do'. Assessed work, whether coursework or final examinations, must enable candidates to show positive achievement. The emphasis is to enable students to show what they can do rather than what they cannot do. GCSE also demands that candidates demonstrate a wider range of skills than did O level or CSE examinations. Not only should candidates be able to recall knowledge, but they should also shows skills of understanding, application, analysis and evaluation. No more than 40 per cent of marks may be allocated to recall of knowledge. At least 20 per cent of the marks must be allocated to coursework. Thus a final examination may be no more than 80 per cent of the marks awarded.[1]

Economics at GCSE

Economics is one of the 22 subjects for which there are National Criteria . In 1990, 28,168 candidates were examined in GCSE Economics. This compares with 59,177 for Business Studies, 219,922 for History, 219,085 for Biology and 659,386 for English.[2] Statistics are not available for candidate entries by age, but these statistics would indicate that fewer than 5 per cent of pupils at age 16 are entered for a GCSE in Economics. The quality of candidates taking GCSE Economics is probably above the national average. In 1989, 51.6 per cent of candidates taking Economics gained a grade C or above. This compares with 42.5 per cent for Business Studies, 47.9 per cent for History, 45.9 per cent for Biology and 48.2 per cent for English Language. More males than females study GCSE Economics. In 1989, 61.1 per cent of those entered for the examination were males whilst only 38.9 per cent were females. This gender bias contrasts with the entry figures for Business Studies and Commerce, where more females than males are entered at GCSE.[3]

All six GCSE groups offer mode 1 syllabuses in Economics. The Southern Examining Group (SEG), with the largest number of candidate entries in 1989, offers an option in their mode 1 syllabus. Candidates have to study a core and then may opt to study either Social Economics or Economic Principles. The Northern Examining Association (NEA) offers two syllabuses, Syllabus A devised for 16-year-olds, and Syllabus B, devised for 'mature candidates' post-16. Apart from the Northern Ireland Examinations Council (NIEC) syllabus and NEA syllabus B, all mode 1 syllabuses have common papers for all candidates. NIEC and NEA Syllabus B have differentiated papers. In the case of the NEA, all candidates must sit Paper 1, which is a limited grade paper to grade C. Any candidate wishing to gain a grade B or A must also sit Paper 2.

The National Criteria for Economics stipulate that syllabuses must require candidates to display a broad range of skills. For instance, courses should enable students to develop 'basic economic numeracy and literacy'. Candidates are expected not only to 'demonstrate recall of knowledge' but also 'demonstrate an ability to use this knowledge . . . demonstrate an ability and apply appropriate terminology, concepts and elementary theories . . . select, analyse, interpret and apply data . . . make reasoned judgements' (DES, 1985a). At least 20 per cent of total marks must be accounted for by data response questions. Hence, most questions on examination papers tend to start with a piece of data and questions are then set on the data or are related to the data.

Basic skills

The assessment objectives in GCSE National Criteria are based upon a Bloomian taxonomy of skills (Bloom *et al.*, 1956). It is sometimes useful to classify these skills into 'lower order' skills, such as knowledge and comprehension, and 'higher order' skills such as application, analysis and evaluation.

Traditional didactic teaching has a place in imparting lower order skills to students. A well structured lecture mixed with questions is an excellent means of introducing economic concepts and theory to pupils. All mode 1 GCSE Economics syllabuses cover both micro-economics and macro-economics. Students are expected to be able to recall concepts ranging from opportunity cost to capital to national income.

Traditional methods of reinforcing understanding of concepts and theories also have a place. Short answer questions are used by some of the examination groups as a means of assessment, whilst MEG uses multiple choice questions. Mathematical questions, based upon hypothetical data, such as simple calculations of profit or loss, or balance of payments surpluses or deficits, can be used too. Teachers may also wish to practise basic presentational skills such as drawing pie charts or graphs.

However, it is arguably better to reinforce economic understanding through selective use of real data wherever possible. There is a plethora of such material available commercially in textbooks, workbooks and packs (see

Chapter 18 in this volume). All published material suffers from two disadvantages. First, the material is inevitably at least a year old when used and is normally several years old. The passage of time often lessens the impact of the data and sometimes makes it impossible to use. This is much more of a problem with macro-economic data than micro-economic data. Second, material published for a national market is most unlikely to cover local issues. The Economics National Criteria specify that students should 'develop a knowledge and understanding of . . . individuals, groups and organisations within the local . . . community'. The study of local issues is an important way in which students come to appreciate that Economics is a discipline which can help them understand the world in which they live. Teachers should, therefore, wherever possible, use material which they themselves have collected recently. Local and national newspapers, magazines, current radio and television broadcasts are all possible sources.

When considering the suitability of material, it is important to remember another requirement of GCSE. With O level and CSE, 'it has not been unusual for the written material given to students to be well beyond their probable reading attainment' (Mobley, 1987). However, it is stated in the General Criteria of GCSE that 'the language used in question papers . . . must be clear, precise and intelligible to candidates throughout the range of entry for the examination' (DES, 1985b). The means of communication used, whether words or graphs or diagrams, must be accessible to F grade candidates if there are F grade candidates in a class or examination room. So material from the *Sun* or the *Daily Mirror*, with a reading age of 9 or 10, would be suitable for presentation to a whole group containing some F grade candidates, whilst material from the *Financial Times* or *The Guardian* would not. In general, only very short extracts taken from quality newspapers are suitable for classroom use at GCSE. Longer extracts need to be rewritten to reduce the reading age of the piece to make it accessible to students. Similarly with television and radio programmes: shorter programmes aimed at a wide audience will be more accessible to students than longer programmes aimed at more sophisticated viewers.

Language is important too when devising tasks. Questions, whether oral or written, should be as simple and direct as possible. Words like 'analyse' or 'evaluate' will not be understood by the vast majority of candidates at this level. On the other hand, appropriate responses can be obtained using phrases such as 'Would it be better if . . . Give reasons for your answer', or 'Is this fair? Support your views with evidence and economic reasoning'.

Higher order skills

Work in basic skills has an important place in teaching economics at GCSE, but teachers need to move beyond this if they are to satisfy the requirements of the National Criteria and make their courses exciting and interesting for their students.

One of the most important ways in which higher order skills can be taught is through the use of decision-making exercises. To come to an economic decision, students need to know some economic facts and economic principles. They need to be able to interpret information which is presented to them, perhaps orally, or in written form, or as statistics. They need to be able to apply their knowledge and understanding in order to interpret and analyse data. They need to be able to select what is important and what is unimportant and distinguish between evidence and opinion. Finally they need to be able to evaluate the evidence to come to a conclusion and present their findings in an accurate and logical manner.

There is a wide variety of decision-making exercises available commercially. Many are games or simulations. For instance, in 'Fares Fair' (Butters and Riley, 1988) students are placed in the roles of management consultants, trade unionists and townspeople and have to make policy recommendations concerning the present subsidised bus service in a town. In 'Redwards Engineering' (Anderton, 1988) students play the roles of trade unionists and management negotiating over a variety of industrial relations problems. These are listed in more detail in Chapter 15.

Another very important way in which candidates can display higher order skills is through the completion of GCSE coursework.

Coursework

Compulsory coursework is a feature of the system of examining at GCSE. Coursework can take many different forms. At one extreme is the project or dissertation. This is a piece of work which is completed in isolation from the rest of the course: the coursework is 'bolted on'. For instance, candidates may work at a 3000 word project over a number of months towards the end of their course, and the topic chosen may have nothing to do with work currently being done in class. At the other extreme is the piece of work which has been completed as a part of a normal programme of studies and which is selected for marking. Coursework in this model is an integral part of the course.

In practice, most teachers will organize their coursework in a way which falls between these two extremes. In part, this decision will be influenced by the requirements of their particular examination group. For instance, the Economics syllabus of the Midland Examining Group (MEG) requires candidates to complete three out of five prescribed topics. These cover second-hand cars, local unemployment, the classification of business functions, the Local Authority budget and a comparison of shop prices. It is likely that teachers will set the coursework tasks at appropriate points in the course: for instance, second-hand cars after having covered price determination or perhaps the behaviour of firms; local unemployment after having taught unemployment and other macro-economic problems; and business functions after having taught the behaviour of firms.

The SEG syllabus is less prescriptive. For instance, those taking the Economics Principles option must complete two pieces of coursework, one a national/international problem or issue, the other a study of a business organization's economic decision-making. This leaves open the possibility of pupils being asked to complete coursework out of context towards the end of their course, but it is more logical for teachers to integrate the coursework with the teaching syllabus.

The Northern Examining Association (NEA) syllabus A gives even greater flexibility. Candidates may choose to submit one, two or three assignments chosen from any area of the syllabus. This syllabus is likely to prove most attractive to those teachers who wish to bolt on coursework to their existing schemes of work.

All the examination groups give examples of coursework to be completed and there are a number of books and packs commercially available which give many more, so neither teacher nor pupil should be short of ideas for coursework.

More difficult can be the completion of coursework to the requirements of the syllabus. Centres have to mark coursework according to assessment criteria. NEA Syllabus A is not untypical in breaking this down into three sets of skills. First, candidates must show that they can recognize, select and present relevant data. The data presented may either be primary data or secondary data. For instance, pupils might have surveyed all the shops in a local shopping centre, detailing their names, what they sell, and noting down prices of selected goods. Another candidate might have followed a particular news story through collecting cuttings from newspapers. Second, candidates must analyse and interpret the data and apply them in an appropriate way. For instance, they should be able to group shops together into types, and ought to be able to explain how shops compete with each other in a local area. Application of economic concepts is generally expected. Third, candidates must make reasoned judgements based on economic principles. For instance, pupils should be able to assess which shops are competing successfully in the local area, and which are less successful.

Many teachers find it difficult to know how much help they should give their students with coursework. On the one hand, it is not right that candidates should be left to get on with coursework totally unaided. On the other hand, teachers should not write the coursework for the candidates.[4] Certainly teachers must explain the criteria by which students will be assessed, and all candidates should be given a copy of the assessment criteria. Teachers should also give guidance to candidates on the choice of topics where choice is available. For instance, no ordinary pupil should be allowed to undertake coursework on 'The Stock Exchange', a classic project topic where in practice candidates do no more than copy out Stock Exchange booklets. Rather, the teacher needs to build up a fund of knowledge about which coursework titles are likely to enable candidates to display the range of skills required. This is likely to involve knowledge of which local firms are helpful, what is suitable for study in the local economic environment and what it is possible to research meaningfully at a national and international level. What is suitable for one candidate is not necessarily suitable for another. A grade A candidate, for instance, needs scope to be able to display the full range of skills required.

Much weaker candidates are unlikely to be able to score highly on analysis and evaluation but, with some guidance, may be able to score very highly on research and presentation of data.

Practical problems

Teaching GCSE Economics presents a number of problems. In most schools, the numbers taking GCSE Economics or the option patterns will necessitate mixed ability teaching. Teachers will respond to this to some extent by setting different work to different pupils. For instance, with coursework, A grade candidates may be guided into a complex study which enables them to display a wide range of skills. Weaker candidates may be guided into simpler studies where they may gain high marks for research but relatively low marks for application and evaluation. Equally, a teacher may set extra homework which is to be completed only by those candidates aspiring to gain a grade C or above. In class, the teacher may have prepared two sets of data, one the original data, the other a simpler adapted version with common questions or perhaps slightly different questions. This last strategy enables all pupils to share in a common experience, so that the teacher can discuss the data with the whole group.

One simple strategy is to set open-ended tasks which enable students to respond at their own different levels. In examining terms, this is known as 'differentiation by outcome'. For instance, students could be asked to examine the Budget. They could be asked to describe the changes presented using newspaper reports. They could then be asked to analyse the effects of the Budget on individuals, businesses and the economy as a whole. Then they could be challenged to evaluate the Budget. Was it a good Budget and what criteria might be used in coming to any conclusions?

The teaching room is of vital importance to effective teaching. Furniture should be flexible, enabling students to work on their own, in small groups or as one large group. There should be easy access to video and other audio-visual equipment, as well as to computers. There should be plenty of wall space to display the students' own work. Equally, the Economics department should be well equipped with other resources. A good textbook, supplementary published materials, original source material, a library of reference books and teacher-produced resources are essential for lively and interesting teaching. In practice, resources are a major constraint for many Economics teachers. They teach in unsuitable rooms, have difficulty gaining access to facilities such as computers, and operate on budgets which are woefully inadequate for their needs.

The attitude of senior management in schools can also present problems. Coursework often requires that students be allowed out of class, perhaps into other areas of the school or out of school altogether. It is unfortunately true that in some schools, senior management discourages teachers from releasing pupils from the classroom at any time.

GCSE Economics and the National Curriculum

Unfortunately, Economics is neither a core nor foundation subject in the National Curriculum, but has been relegated to the footnotes by being designated a cross-curricular theme. With many secondary schools thinking of moving towards a 90 per cent or even 100 per cent National Curriculum timetable, it might seem that GCSE Economics will be squeezed out of the curriculum altogether. It should be remembered, though, that GCSE Economics has always been a last or near-last choice for pupils opting at age 14. There were relatively few schools which did not encourage if not force their 14-year-old pupils, particularly the more able, to study one if not two sciences, a modern language, an art or craft subject and perhaps history or geography. So long as schools run at least one option pool, the competitive pressure on Economics is unlikely to be much greater than it was before the advent of the National Curriculum. Moreover, a significant number of entries[5] come from sixth forms and further education colleges, which will be unaffected by the National Curriculum.

The threat to the survival of GCSE Economics comes from closer quarters. A variety of GCSE syllabuses will be devised in the early 1990s to cover the requirements of Technology, one of the foundation subjects. Technology contains some elements of Business Studies. It could be that many schools will opt to enter their candidates for a GCSE in the Craft, Design and Technology (CDT) area and a GCSE in Business Studies or Business and Information Studies. If the school offers a GCSE in Business Studies, then it is unlikely to offer a GCSE in Economics. It could be that GCSE Business Studies will replace GCSE Economics in the 14–16 curriculum. This would be unfortunate given the unique contribution the study of Economics can make to the child's growing perception of the adult world.

Notes

1. Temporary dispension for coursework was initially given to Mathematics.
2. Provisional results from the Joint Council for the General Certificate of Secondary Education.
3. Inter-group statistics Summer 1989, The Joint Council for the General Certificate of Secondary Education.
4. The 1989 MEG examiners' report stated: 'This year a number of centres appear to have given far too much "help" to their candidates. This has taken the form of what can only be described as a dot-to-dot approach. Candidates are issued with course work booklets in which they fill in the blanks. It is hard to see how such work can be the individual work of the candidate. Of course the teacher must advise, counsel and supervise the students but this is not the same as writing it for them. In most cases such help seems to have restricted the most able and limited their grade chances'.
5. It is not possible to say how many because the examination groups do not release figures for entry by age.

References

Anderton, A (1988) 'Redwards Engineering', in Whitehead, DJ (ed.) *Trade-Offs*. Longman, Harlow.

Bloom, BS *et al*. (1956) *Taxonomy of Educational Objectives. Handbook 1. Cognitive Domain*. Longman, Harlow.

Butters, K and Riley, C (1988) 'Fairs Fair', in Whitehead, DJ (ed.) *Trade-Offs*. Longman, Harlow.

DES (1985a) *GCSE. The National Criteria. Economics*. HMSO, London.

DES (1985b) *GCSE. General Criteria*. HMSO, London.

Mobley, M (1987) *Making Ourselves Clearer. Readibility in the GCSE*. Working Paper 5, Secondary Examinations Council, London.

4 The Establishment of Economic and Industrial Understanding as a Cross-curricular Theme within the National Curriculum in England

Anna Craft and Ian Pearce

Introduction

This chapter outlines the process which was involved in establishing economic and industrial understanding as an entitlement within the National Curriculum of England in the form of a cross-curricular theme. The National Curriculum Council's project, 'Educating for Economic Awareness', set up by the School Curriculum Development Committee (later superseded by the National Curriculum Council) in July 1987, played a key coordinating role in this process.

SCDC sets up 'Educating for Economic Awareness'

The establishment of a curriculum development project, funded jointly by education and industry, working in over 40 Local Education Authorities, came in response to a consultative letter issued by Sir Keith Joseph (then Minister for Education) in March 1985. The letter outlined various proposals for the inclusion of economic awareness within the school curriculum using a cross-curricular approach, rather than a separate subject model, and for curriculum development. The response to this letter, from many educational bodies and associations, led to the establishment of a curriculum development project under the School Curriculum Development Committee. It was founded on 14 principles, developed by a consultation group after a planning conference (SCDC, 1986) (see Table 4.1).

The planning/consultation group drew on HMI evidence collected during a 1985 survey on economic understanding in the school curriculum (HMI, 1985). Although it was concerned mainly with the 14–16 age range, the

1. 'Economic Awareness' refers to a continuum that begins with economic awareness, progressing through economic understanding to economic competence and capability.
2. Economic Awareness should permeate the curriculum for the full age range 5–16/18 and the full ability range including those with special educational needs, as a part of general education.
3. Its purpose is to enable young people to make informed decisions throughout their lives.
4. It must equip young people for their roles as producers, consumers and citizens.
5. Economic awareness should be defined in terms of concepts, knowledge, skills and attitudes and it should include moral, ethical and political dimensions.
6. Delivery should be achieved within schools by strategies of permeation and integration; coordination of team approaches will be important, implying the appointment of school coordinators and attention to the management of change.
7. Experiential learning should predominate although the focus should not be purely local, but also regional, national and global.
8. Teacher awareness and the need for a minimum theoretical background should be prioritized, through teacher-led school-based INSET with external support, and initial teacher education.
9. There is a need for further materials development including worksheets, texts, video tapes/discs and simulation activities.
10. Genuine partnerships between education and industry should be established.
11. Parents and the wider community surrounding schools should be involved.
12. Continuity of education should be developed, within and between schools.
13. Methods of assessment should be explored, including profiling.
14. It should undertake to coordinate the initiatives in this field.

Table 4.1 *The 14 principles on which 'Educating for Economic Awareness' was founded, developed by the consultation group in July 1986*

inspection also covered practice with older and younger pupils. Amongst other things, the HMI report commented on several different curricular models of provision for economic understanding in schools as follows:

• Examinable courses in subjects whose structure and content were directly concerned with aspects of economic understanding (for example, economics and business studies). These were usually optional courses and in the 14–16 and 16–18 age ranges.

HMI comment: Lessons were more effective when they went beyond the mere transmission of information and became genuine attempts to extend the understanding of pupils, using a variety of teaching techniques and offering good opportunities for oral expression, with suitably high expectations of pupils' performance. In some schools, the curriculum development work in preparation for core economics modules had raised the

awareness of teachers to alternative approaches to teaching, which had enhanced provision within optional courses.
- Core modules in economic understanding (for example, as part of PSE courses).

HMI comment: Although they represented a positive step in the provision of economic understanding, they were frequently confined to limited themes such as consumer education, personal budgeting and industrial enterprise, without reference to wider objectives of economic understanding. Successful core lessons in economic understanding were characterised by active learning approaches, effective supporting materials, much oral involvement by pupils, variety and pace during the lesson, appropriate expectations and enthusiastic teachers who were well matched, in terms of their qualifications or experience, to the teaching task. There was, nevertheless, scope for the development of more appropriate teaching styles and materials and for inservice training to encourage and support such developments.
- Related subjects such as geography, social studies and CDT, which make contributions to economic understanding although their main fields of interest lie elsewhere.

HMI comment: Evidence collected demonstrated that aspects of economic understanding could be effectively dealt with through the study of other subjects and also through pre-vocational courses. Nevertheless, the management of this potential for developing economic understanding across the curriculum remained unco-ordinated and undeveloped; more remained to be done to raise consciousness among teachers about the contribution that their subjects could make.
- Other activities, such as work experience and the running of mini-enterprises, which contributed to economic understanding, but were not located in any particular subject.

HMI comment: Although pupils who had been involved in activities such as those above were often enthusiastic about their experiences and knowledgeable in certain fields, such as setting up and running a business, the activities tended to be too narrow in themselves to address all the objectives of economic understanding. Poor planning and evaluation had meant that for some pupils, their experiences were counterproductively demotivating.

From July 1987, SCDC's 'Educating for Economic Awareness' carried out a national survey covering the whole age range, 5–16 and identified areas of need for curriculum development which did not duplicate the work of other major projects (for example, business education in the secondary phase, which was being widely supported by the TVEI through a variety of measures, and industry education, which was being developed by SCIP, UBI and Industry Matters). With these findings in mind, and working with the government's early documents outlining the structure of the National Curriculum, EEA set up local curriculum development projects in a range of LEAs, each with a local coordinator (some part time, some full time) and most in collaboration with a link/support project within the field of economic and industrial understanding, with whom much of the development work in schools was carried out. In all, projects were set up on 42 LEAs, involving 465 schools and 4154 teachers in several areas of curriculum development (see table 4.2).

---

1. Whole school curriculum and related issues including management and coordination, and cross-curricular provision.
2. Specific foundation subjects, including science, technology, information technology, mathematics, English, geography.
3. Specific areas of economic and industrial understanding, including primary consumer education, global issues and trade union education.
4. Separate provision for economic and industrial understanding through personal and social education.
5. Development work and partnership across the curriculum arising from teacher placements in industry.

Table 4.2 *Areas of curriculum development in local 'Educating for Economic Awareness' projects*

For schools, economic awareness meant bringing actual economic problems and issues into relevant curricular slots in primary and secondary topics, subjects and modules. The curricular aims of Educating for Economic Awareness were to equip all young people with:

- the UNDERSTANDING of basic economic ideas, such as scarcity of resources, wealth creation and distribution;
- the COMPETENCE to apply appropriate knowledge, concepts and skills of critical review and analysis to economic issues and problems so that balanced and informed decisions are made with due regard to evidence, moral values and social responsibility;
- the CAPABILITY to participate positively as a producer, consumer and citizen in adult society, able to identify and evaluate the economic aspects of decision making at all levels – from individual and family affairs to the workplace and community at large including national and global issues (SCDC, 1987).

The project also published guidance on the meaning of economic awareness, which stressed the unity between knowledge-based perspectives (eg economics education), procedure-based perspectives (eg process of critical enquiry) and needs-based perspectives (eg business education, consumer education, industry education and the work-related curriculum) (Pearce, 1989). During the course of the three and a half years of the project's life, from May 1987 to December 1990, NCC took the place of SCDC. The project played a substantial role in advising the Council, especially its Whole Curriculum Committee, on cross-curricular themes and then in organizing the working party which advised NCC on practical curriculum guidance on economic and industrial understanding across the school curriculum for pupils aged 5–16. The original remit of the project allowed for this, as shown in Table 4.3.

---

1. *Provide national coordination and support* for all curriculum development and training work promoting Economic and Industrial Understanding across the National Curriculum and whole school curriculum for all young people 5–16;

    Action taken: Set up a national network for all organisations promoting economic and industrial understanding; provided consultancy and INSET to LEAs, schools and other projects nationwide; advised government, NCC, industry, and education on EIU 5–16/19 years.

2. *Undertake collaborative curriculum development* in researched areas of need for the provision of Economic and Industrial Understanding as a cross-curricular theme in the National Curriculum and whole school curriculum;

    Action taken: collaborative projects involving all main organisations in EIU including SCIP, GSIP, MEIAP, EcATT working in over 40 LEAs with sponsorship from industry.

3. *Research the theoretical framework* for Economic and Industrial Understanding as a cross-curricular theme developing knowledge, skills and understanding through the four key stages of the National Curriculum;

    Action taken: published guidance on the meaning of economic awareness; researched conceptual development, teaching methods and curriculum provision in UK and other nations.

4. *Develop guidelines/Non-Statutory Guidance* for schools providing exemplified strategies for curricular provision in both National Curriculum foundation subjects and in topics, thematic studies, consolidation programmes and PSE, together with policies for the management and co-ordination of Economic and Industrial Understanding as a cross-curricular theme;

    Action taken: co-ordination of the preparation of *Curriculum Guidance 4: Education for Economic and Industrial Understanding*; also two sets of INSET materials to go free to all schools; one on EIU in the Primary School and one on the management and co-ordination of EIU as a cross curricular theme. Preparation of publicity poster and curriculum guidance on teacher placements as a form of staff/curriculum development and preparation of classroom materials in consumer education for Key Stages 1 and 2. Numerous LEA level publications.

5. Inform and advise NCC professional officers and Council members on the provision of Economic and Industrial Understanding in the school curriculum 5–16 and undertake NCC committee, task group and consultation work.	Action taken: Advised NCC on cross-curricular themes, skills, EIU in National Curriculum foundation subjects and industry and business partnerships and the National Curriculum.

Table 4.3 *The remit of the Educating for Economic Awareness Project, together with action taken*

Source: *Economic and Industrial Understanding as a Cross-curricular theme in the National Curriculum: Curriculum Guidance 4.*

In April 1990, advice on economic and industrial understanding as a cross-curricular theme was published by NCC, in *Curriculum Guidance 4: Education for Economic and Industrial Understanding.* It stated that education for economic and industrial understanding is clearly required if schools are to provide a curriculum which promotes the aims defined in the Education Reform Act. NCC's view is that as a cross-curricular theme, economic and industrial understanding contributes to personal and social development by preparing pupils for the economic decisions they face in their present and future lives; as producers, consumers and citizens in a democracy. *Curriculum Guidance 4* specifies that it can be taught through foundation subjects and other areas of the whole curriculum. Aspects of economic and industrial understanding are embedded in the statutory orders for some subjects, for example industry and the environment in science; marketing and consumer choice in technology. Other aspects provide important contexts relevant to pupils' lives through which subject knowledge and skills can be developed, for example managing finances in mathematics and debating controversial issues in English. Future foundation subjects, eg history, geography and modern foreign languages, will include aspects of this theme.

NCC recommends that Local Education Authorities and schools should review and develop their policies for promoting economic and industrial understanding, which should be based on the following principles:

- A broad and balanced programme – covering all aspects of economic and industrial understanding relevant to the lives of pupils, such as business, commerce, financial management, organization of industry and industrial relations, consumer education, impact of technology on work and lifestyles, the national and global economy and the role of government and international organizations; pupils should be encouraged to debate controversial issues in a balanced way and to explore values and beliefs, both their own and others'.

- Knowledge, understanding, skills and attitudes – pupils need to know and understand certain basic economic concepts, for example the idea that making economic decisions should involve an analysis of costs and benefits; they also need skills to investigate and analyse economic issues, make judgements and take decisions; in addition they should develop the attitudes needed to participate responsibly in adult life (see Table 4.4).

- Direct experience of industry and the world of work – pupils in all key stages should visit and investigate industries and other places of work and have opportunities to talk and work with adults from industry and the community, including employers and trade unionists; for older pupils, economic and industrial understanding should be linked to careers education and guidance and (for pupils aged 15 and over) work experience placements.

- Involvement in business and community enterprise – education for enterprise means developing the qualities needed to be an enterprising person, such as the ability to tackle problems and work in teams, and taking part in small-scale business and community enterprises which help develop an understanding of business and wealth creation as well as community work.

- Access for all pupils – all pupils, regardless of culture, gender and social background should have access to a curriculum which promotes economic and industrial understanding; schools should be aware of pupils' attitudes and assumptions and challenge stereotypes such as gender stereotypes about the study of technology and engineering as a career; in line with NCC's *Curriculum Guidance 2 – A Curriculum for All*, activities should be carefully planned to allow access for pupils with special learning needs.

- A record of pupils' experiences and achievements – schools should consider ways of recording pupils' experiences in economic and industrial understanding; assessment in all relevant parts of the curriculum should take these into account and schools may wish to include these in each pupil's record of achievement.

- Provision across the whole curriculum 5–16 – economic and industrial understanding can be developed in most subjects; for example, economic data can be used to promote mathematical skills, or an industrial context used to study scientific or technological processes. It is likely that schools will plan provision largely within foundation subjects, whether these are taught in an integrated way, as in some primary schools, or as separate subjects. No single subject can provide the full range of knowledge, understanding and skills required by this cross-curricular theme, but some subjects, such as technology, science and geography, are more important than others; for example, the programmes of study for technology specify business and industry as a context for design and technological change. Aspects of economic and industrial understanding can be taught alongside other cross-curricular themes; for example, consumer choices about diet raise health issues, knowing about alternative economic policies is essential for future citizenship and knowing about the impact of economic decisions upon the environment links with both health and citizenship. Schools may wish to consider supplementary provision alongside foundation subjects, through blocks of time focused on specific tasks, such as enterprise activities or study weeks, separately timetabled programmes for Personal

Knowledge and understanding of:

- key economic concepts, such as production, distribution, supply and demand
- how business enterprise creates wealth for individuals and the community
- the organization of industry and industrial relations
- what it means to be a consumer, how consumer decisions are made and the implications of these decisions
- the relationship between economy and society in different economic systems
- technological developments and their impact on lifestyles and workplaces
- the role of government and international organizations (for example, the European Community) in regulating the economy and providing public services.

Analytical, personal and social skills, including the ability to:

- collect, analyse and interpret economic and industrial data
- think carefully about different ways of solving economic problems and making decisions
- distinguish between statements of fact and value in economic situations
- communicate economic ideas accurately and clearly
- establish working relationships with adults outside school
- cooperate as part of a team in enterprise activities
- lead and take the initiative
- handle differences of opinion in a group
- communicate effectively and listen to the views of others on economic and industrial issues.

Attitudes, including

- an interest in economic and industrial affairs
- respect for evidence and rational argument in economic contexts
- concern for the use of scarce resources
- a sense of responsibility for the consequences of their own economic actions, as individuals and members of groups
- sensitivity to the effects of economic choices on the environment
- concern for human rights, as these are affected by economic decisions.

Table 4.4 *A summary of the knowledge, understanding, skills and attitudes involved in economic and industrial understanding given in NCC's* Curriculum Guidance 4: Education for Economic and Industrial Understanding

and Social Education and separate consolidation modules on economic and industrial understanding.
- Progression and continuity 5–16 – schools need to plan carefully to provide a continuous and progressive programme of activities across the curriculum for every pupil, avoiding unnecessary duplication. NCC's *Curriculum Guidance 4* suggests ways in which economic and industrial understanding might be taught at each key stage in relation to appropriate programmes of study and attainment targets and other areas of the school curriculum (see table 4.5, for examples).

KEY STAGE 1	KEY STAGE 2	KEY STAGE 3	KEY STAGE 4
Economic Concepts			
Make decisions about using resources in the classroom, eg materials for a model	Understand the implications of limited resources, eg equipment bought with a limited budget	Decision making and scarcity of available resources, eg funding for roads and/or health	Scarcity means making choices between alternatives analysing the implications, eg the social costs and benefits of alternative hospital budgets
Business Enterprise			
Understand how simple goods are produced using resources, eg materials, tools and assembly in a factory	Understand how goods are produced, distributed and sold, eg study how a factory makes and sells goods	Relationship between market research, production and sales, eg survey wants and calculate costs/price	Business action plans which relate costs to forecasts of production levels and revenue, eg mini-enterprise activity
Industry and Work			
Describe different kinds of work eg work of adults in school	Understand work places and work roles, eg work in local services and industry	Investigate specialist roles, eg the role of managers in industry	Understand people's rights and responsibilities at work, eg health and safety regulations and equal opportunities laws
Consumer Education			
Be aware that people are consumers of goods and services, eg local shops, buses and libraries	Understand what it means to be an informed consumer, eg examine the idea of value for money	Consumer preference and design, packaging and advertising, eg marketing of low-pollutant safer cars	Consumer decisions depend on price, value, quality, advertising and personal wealth, eg explore how consumer patterns relate to wealth patterns

Table 4.5 *Examples of progression within economic and industrial understanding*

- Management and coordination – to ensure that provision across the whole curriculum is part of a coherent programme, careful planning and monitoring will be required; schools should map aspects of economic and industrial understanding as part of their audit of the whole curriculum and develop an action plan linking this theme to other cross-curricular elements as a systematic entitlement for every pupil taught through foundation and other subjects and supplementary studies. As part of this whole-school policy, INSET needs should be identified and appropriate provision made. Many schools are involved in Compacts, school–industry links and education–business partnerships which support provision for economic and industrial understanding by providing workplaces to visit, industrialists in the classroom and placements for pupils and teachers.

Case studies of possible activities promoting economic and industrial understanding in each key stage were included in *Curriculum Guidance 4*. These were based on current practice developed by the 'Educating for Economic Awareness' project and other organizations promoting this theme in schools; these case studies emphasize the process of active enquiry and experiential learning which foster the development of knowledge and understanding, skills and attitudes.

In *Curriculum Guidance 4*, NCC views economic and industrial understanding as a requirement. All teachers should recognize their responsibility for developing appropriate aspects of this cross-curricular theme as part of their corporate contribution to a broadly based, balanced and relevant whole curriculum. All schools should plan systematic provision across their whole curriculum, carefully monitored to ensure that every pupil is prepared for the challenges of adult life as producers, consumers and citizens.

Conclusions

The last three years have offered the opportunity for those educationalists and others in the community who believe that every child requires economic and industrial understanding to prepare them to make informed and responsible decisions as producers, consumers and citizens in adult life, to make this theme an entitlement in law. As NCC's *Curriculum Guidance 4* states, 'Economic and industrial understanding is clearly required if schools are to provide a curriculum which promotes the aims defined in the Education Reform Act' (NCC, 1990). NCC's 'Educating for Economic Awareness' project has been fortunate to play a national role in coordinating the work of over thirty other initiatives and working with teachers and collaborating projects nationwide, to help prepare a coherent and unified guidance on how schools can make provision for economic and industrial understanding for every child, 5–16.

The evaluation report on the project, prepared by Dr Jon Nixon at the University of Sheffield, Division of Education, noted the achievements in consultancy, INSET, networking, published materials and advice to NCC and others in the field. It also highlighted a number of strategies which are critical for cross-curricular provision; these include:

- Developing supportive, professional groups of teachers within and across schools and phases.

- Building school management structures that foster corporate responsibility, coordinate the curriculum and facilitate collaborative work.
- Planning a coherent and clearly articulated system of LEA-wide support for curriculum review and development.
- Establishing national and local forums in which teachers and organizations committed to EIU can share ideas and concerns.

The report goes on to call for a continuing unit within NCC to further develop EIU across the whole curriculum of all schools and to maintain the network of agencies, projects and organizations currently supporting schools. NCC is planning to set up an industry unit to take on this further work. The project team will publish INSET packs on the primary curriculum and the management and co-ordination of economic and industrial understanding. In addition, the team, in partnership with other organizations such as SCIP, SATRO and ASE, are preparing further guidance and INSET packs for EIU in foundation subjects and work experience programmes, together with a booklet on the advantages of teacher placements in industry as a form of staff development.

Economic and industrial understanding is no longer an optional part of the curriculum, championed by enthusiasts. With the help of collaborating projects throughout the country, it has now become an entitlement for every child.

References

HMI (1985) *Economic Understanding in the School Curriculum*. HMSO, London.

Pearce, I (1989) 'Putting perspectives in perspective', *Forum* (NCC), republished in *Economics* 25, Pt 1

NCC (1990) *Curriculum Guidance 4: Education for Economic and Industrial Understanding*. National Curriculum Council, York.

SCDC (1986) *Planning Conference on Economic Awareness*. SCDC, London.

SCDC (1987) *Curriculum Issues No. 4, Educating for Economic Awareness: A Basic Entitlement in the School Curriculum*. SCDC, London.

5 Economics Education for All

Steve Hodkinson and Linda Thomas

The Economic Awareness Teacher Training Programme (EcATT), a partnership between two universities, industry, commerce, research trusts, and central and local government, was established in 1986. This chapter is a brief account of some aspects of its work to promote economics education within the entitlement curriculum for all young people.

Definition

We have adopted the term 'economic awareness' to signify our intention of helping pupils to become conscious or aware of their own way of thinking about economic phenomena and of the existence of different and more helpful ways. As we reported in the TES (Hodkinson and Thomas, 1989) the results of research and curriculum development work since the early 1970s[1] had convinced us that

> Young people's experiences of the economic system come from many sources. The media is a major one bombarding them with information and conclusions. Activities such as shopping, choosing, giving, contributing, building, throwing away, working, making, allocating time and resources, sharing, selling and seeing people in need provide experiences in a range of contexts. As a result young people develop an intuitive feel for the economic system – their own commonsense rules. Their behaviour, what they do, how they act and the decisions they make are then influenced, even determined, by those perceptions or knowledge. It is possible to become skilled at operating in this way to appear to develop a degree of confidence as certain courses of action are reinforced. It is equally possible to become a pawn, controlled by, rather than in control of, the system. In neither case is true understanding achieved.

We are convinced that any programme purporting to contribute to economics education needs to take this into account. Unless pupils are enabled consciously to examine and review their interpretation of their economics experiences and their understanding of the economic system, there can be no guarantee that they will develop a real feel for the way the economic system works, how it affects their lives and how it might be affected.

Thus, in our view, the task of defining economic awareness involves more than listing key concepts, knowledge, skills; it means more than specifying useful contexts for investigation. We have been concerned to define the economics education entitlement as a relationship between theory and experience, the means for pupils to *engage* their experiences and to examine and review their interpretation. This means that we place considerable emphasis on classrooms as the obvious source of data about the effect of the teacher's intention on pupil outcomes. Teachers working with EcATT attempt to make their intentions explicit during planning and, where possible to phrase them in terms of the form of understanding they wish to promote. During lessons they endeavour to concentrate on evidence of pupils' intentions and of the meanings assigned by them to the experiences and phenomena. Written and verbal accounts of lessons provide data for the collaborative review of teacher and pupil intentions and meanings and of the success of the learning experiences.

The use of this collaborative plan/teach/review strategy, a characteristic feature of EcATT's approach, is well documented.[2] It has made it possible to produce statements defining economic awareness, which, because they have been derived from pupils' classroom work by means of a process of shared teacher review and reformulation, represent the preferred form of understanding of situations and phenomena. The statements in Figure 5.1 relate to easily identifiable contexts such as consumer affairs, business, enterprise, etc.[3] Those in Figure 5.2 are drawn from subject-specific work in Science, Mathematics, English etc.[4]

Implications for the curriculum

Economic awareness within subjects

According to the definition of economic awareness presented here, it is important that teachers attempt

> to instil procedures which allow individuals to take a more reflective stance in relation to the events in which they are personally involved (Thomas and Hodkinson, 1988, p.8)

Experience shows that when teachers attempt to help pupils to examine and review their understanding of the economic system it is necessary to canvass the help of knowledge and skills gained in subjects other than economics. The following example illustrates this.

A group of teachers worked together on an activity which invited pupils to place several brands of sausage in order of preference (broadcast in Economic Awareness INSET; BBC, 1988). One teacher introduced the lesson and then explained the task – 'we've bought the sausages . . . we want you to decide which is the best to buy. Put them in rank order from most preferred to least preferred and give the reasons for your choice'. The pupils, working in groups, completed the task of putting the wrappers in order, the rank order was displayed and discussion focused on the differences. Pupils were then told that more information – the backs of the wrappers – was available. They were asked if this would alter their views.

In the context of *consumer decisions* young people should be aware of

- the nature of goods and services and the purpose of consumption
- the demand for goods and its relationship with such things as prices, income levels
- the demand for goods and services and the effects of the availability of information, its quality and the extent of external influences on the demand for goods and services
- the existence of and effect of uncertainty, eg inflation and unemployment
- relationships between changes in the pattern of consumption and structural growth and the responsibility of individuals towards the environment, the diminution of scarce resources, and the community in general
- the nature and functions of institutions which lock the individual into the economic system, eg banks, taxation.

In a *business* context pupils should be aware of

- the nature of enterprise and the purpose of production
- the role of manufacturing and service industries in the production process
- the effects of change and growth in the economic and industrial environment and the implications of new technology
- the range of financial costs involved in production
- the effectiveness of different ways of organizing the production process, the existence of economics of scale, of obstacles to growth and the nature of small business contributions
- the importance of investment and training to the well being of the industrial and commercial sector of the economy
- the causes of conflict and the relationship between different interest groups
- the responsibility of industry and commerce towards the environment, the diminution of scarce resources and the community.

In the context of the *national economy* pupils should be aware of

- alternative methods of organizing the production of community goods and services in terms of costs, efficiency, etc
- the pricing of community goods and services – market and re-distributive exchange
- the effects of community decisions on institutions, both nationally and internationally and on individuals and groups
- alternative valuations of different interest groups and sources of conflict in relation to the notion of consensus
- the responsibility of the community and nation towards the environment and the diminution of scarce resources
- the existence of unemployed resources.

Figure 5.1 *Economic awareness contexts*

	Key Stage I	Key Stage II
(i) Identify and investigate economic activities	Pupils should: • be able to describe a variety of economic activities, in particular those in which they are involved, eg shopping, giving, tending a garden, sharing toys • recognize and be able to name a variety of different jobs using categories or pictures, eg pictures of uniforms • understand some of the connections between different jobs, eg teacher, accountant, shopkeeper	Pupils should: • give examples of a wide variety of economic activities and describe the connections between them, eg. saving, banks/building societies, travelling • know that there are different ways of organizing the production of goods and services, eg food production, waste/sewage, transport • use terms like money, trade, in connection with the organization of economic activity and be aware of their limitations
(ii) Identify and explore the purpose of economic activity	• recognize the motives for the economic activity with which they are mainly in contact, at home and in school, eg voluntary helpers, local shopkeepers, teachers, Macdonalds	• be able to advocate and justify their views about the meaning of terms used in connection with economic activity, eg rewards, (money/other), wealth/welfare costs (money/other)
(iii) Interpret, analyse and appraise quality of information on economic activity	• Use pictures, drawings, real objects to record their own economic activity • handle different criteria such as price, value, cost, worth and use them to classify objects	• recognize that pictures and text may carry more than one message about economic activity, eg adverts • be able to use different terms to describe the activity as appropriate, eg work, leisure
(iv) Identify sources which influence and constrain economic activity	• know what amount of food and water are necessary to sustain life and know that it may be different from the amount consumed	• understand that resources are limited, eg global energy • know that scientific and technological developments can increase the range and amount of goods and services available from given sources • recognize that some economic activity has the same effect as increasing resources
(v) Predict the outcomes and effects of their own and others' economic activity	• make predictions based on experience about the effects of their economic activity, eg saving, throwing away, charity campaigns • ask and respond to the questions 'what would happen if . . .' in relation to economic activities which they might not have experienced, eg what if there were no bus services (in big towns or in the country)	• be able to work out that economic activity has different effects on different people, eg by investigating the Channel Tunnel or the effects of a change in exchange rates
(vi) Critically appraise ways of organizing economic activity, its outcomes and effects	• Organize information from a number of sources to review individual economic actions, eg saving for a treat, borrowing.	• Organize information from a number of sources to review group economic actions, eg mini-enterprise, organizing a Christmas fair.

Figure 5.2 *Economic awareness activities*

	Key Stage II	Key Stage IV
(i) Identify and investigate economic activities	Pupils should: • understand that they engage in economic activity in a number of ways, eg as individual consumers, as owners of resources, as members of a community • be able to form, use and be aware of some of the limitations of the general categories employed to classify and describe the organization of economic activity, eg markets, businesses, retailing, money costs	Pupils should: • appreciate the complexity of every form of economic activity whether within the family context or international setting
(ii) Identify and explore the purpose of economic activity	• distinguish between quality and quantity with regard to the purpose of economic activity • understand the source of conflict between different motives for economic activity, eg planning proposals	• know that some economic activity is aimed at mitigating the effects of a lack of balance between individuals and groups with regard to the ownership of resources, eg trade unions, taxation, free education and health, aid
(iii) Interpret, analyse and appraise quality of information on economic activity	• know that the presentation of information about economic activity in daily newspapers, etc may be inconsistent, inaccurate and biased, eg metaphor, graphical representation • recognize expressions of opinions or personal feelings in the presentation of information about economic activity, eg wage settlements, industrial disputes, trade union activity, local planning issues, mergers/takeovers, taxation	• be familiar with the range of techniques in current use to simplify the presentation of information about complex areas of economic activity, eg inflation, unemployment, GNP, graphs showing rates of change
(iv) Identify sources which influence and constrain economic activity	• know that needs change over time and place • recognize that needs are influenced by many factors, eg by conducting surveys on the influence of adverts and media on teenage markets • know that developments in education and health can improve the quality of the outcomes of economic activity and the quantity of goods and services produced	• ask and respond to such questions as 'on what does society's energy needs depend?' by evaluating their own and other societies' economic activity • recognize sources of inertia in any economic system, eg some institutions, expectations
(v) Predict the outcomes and effects of their own and others' economic activity	• recognize that the link between population growth and decline and availability of resources is a complex one, mediated by science and technology, eg food production	• trace the effects of decisions by groups and communities to pool resources
(vi) Critically appraise ways of organizing economic activity, its outcomes and effects	• organize information from a number of sources to advocate and review their views about some local and national issues, eg use of fertilizers, pollution	• organize information from a number of sources to advocate and review their views about local and national issues, eg the provision of free goods and services, property

Two groups were interested in the ingredients:

P2/3   More E numbers . . . we don't know what they are.
T   What does 'meat' mean? Does it have a lot of fat in it?
P1   There's lots about storing the sausages . . . but not much on what's in them.
P4   What other meats? What does this mean?
P5   Don't know what these E numbers are
P6   What's normal pork and beef?
P4   50/50?

When groups reported back to the whole class for the second time, one group had changed its mind. They were asked to explain:

Gr.4   No . . . the nutrition and cooking instructions were OK . . . but we did ask about Marks and Spencer . . . who actually makes the sausages for Marks and Spencer?
T   Are you asking me? I don't know. I can't tell you that. That might be something you'd like to try and find out.
Gr.3   We've changed our views. You wouldn't have time when shopping and you'd need a degree in nutrition to cope . . . our 'last' one was the same as the 'best' on nutrition. Under pressure we would grab the one with fancy packages.

The teachers came to the conclusion that what they had regarded as a straightforward economics investigation was hindered by their pupils' disinclination to draw on their scientific knowledge in order to utilize the nutritional and consumer information provided.

The importance of other subjects

Evidence such as this has led us to conclude that economic awareness cannot be treated as a neat curricular package (eg as a self-contained curriculum element or module) since assistance from other subjects is often crucial for the full exploitation of learning opportunities. National Curriculum Council reports on the nature and purpose of the core and foundation subjects of the National Curriculum suggest that teachers of subjects other than economics should be able to offer assistance:

Mathematics has a crucial role to play in equipping young people to meet the responsibilities of adult life – as citizens, employees, and members of households (Maths Working Group Report, August 1988, p. 7, para. 14).

Schools have an important role to play in helping children to understand the world they live in (Science Working Group, August 1988, p. 6, para. 2.3).

English contributes to preparation for the adult world: people need to be able to communicate effectively and appropriately in all the widely differing social situations in which they find themselves (English for Ages 5–16 Working Group Report, June 1989, para. 2.14).

History gives pupils a framework of reference for the informed use of leisure, and a critically sharpened intelligence with which to make sense of current affairs (History Working Group – Final Report, 1990, p. 2, para. 1.7).

The specific requirements contained in the Attainment Targets and Programmes of Study for Science, Mathematics and English also demonstrate clearly that opportunities to acquire the understanding necessary for economic awareness exist in the core subjects. The number, algebra, measures and data handling Attainment Targets in Mathematics and the speaking and listening and reading Attainment Targets in English provide such opportunities. In Mathematics, they are components of the ability to analyse and evaluate the numerical, graphical and statistical ways in which information about the economic system is represented. One of the examples used to illustrate Attainment Target 9 is to 'Make a collection of graphs or charts from daily newspapers, consider whether any of them are misleading or could be misinterpreted; discuss how the information could have been presented more clearly'. In English, Programmes of Study at Key Stages 3 and 4 state that pupils should be taught how to analyse documents critically (p. 34). In Science, the knowledge and understanding of science, communication and the applications and implications of Science Attainment Targets are components of the ability critically to appraise ways of organizing economic activity and its outcomes and effects. Some specific attainments in Science are

Know that the impact of human activity on the Earth is relatively recent and understand that it is related to the size of population, economic factors and industrial requirements.

Be able to evaluate the various costs and benefits of different energy sources and appreciate that society needs to take these into account before making decisions on policy.

These all serve as a reminder of the importance for the development of pupils' economic awareness of all sources of knowledge, since they assert that to know a subject means being able to bring that knowledge to bear on the economic, political, social, environmental and technological issues, problems and activities of the modern world.

Economic awareness in the whole curriculum

Time will tell whether or not the National Curriculum will succeed in encouraging teachers of subjects other than Economics to accept responsibility for the development of their pupils' economic awareness. Meantime, pupils may need additional help to integrate knowledge from more than one source because a one-to-one correspondence between subjects and issues/activities is unlikely to exist. The implications for management, while considerable, are anticipated in the NCC's (1989) endorsement of the broad aims of the 1988 Education Reform Act:

Teachers need to collaborate in their whole curriculum planning, especially in analysing attainment targets and interpreting programmes of study (para. 6).

Schools need to ensure that the planned contribution of different subjects is not made in isolation but in the light of their contribution to pupils' learning as a whole (para. 7).

(Teachers) should have a clear view of how their teaching contributes to the whole curriculum experiences of their pupils . . . (They should make links) between what they teach and what their pupils learn at other times . . . (para. 8).

The issues raised are usually described by using the term 'coherence'.

Implications for teachers of Economics

Two crucial questions remain for Economics teachers

- Who is going to ensure that it is possible for subject teachers fully to exploit the opportunities provided by their subjects to contribute to the development of pupils' economic awareness?
- Who is going to tackle the coherence issue?

In our view, in both cases, the teacher of Economics has a crucial role to play.

Working with colleagues

During the last decade Economics teachers have gained considerable experience of working with their colleagues to alert them to the benefits and problems of using contexts with an economic/social dimension in their teaching. Their role has also broadened because of other changes. Schools have responded to invitations to cooperate with an increasing number of agencies to provide experiences for pupils of aspects of the economic system deemed relevant, for example, consumer affairs and the worlds of business, work and enterprise. Economics teachers have sought to ensure a place on the agenda for questions about pupils' *understanding* of work experience, mini-enterprise and other activities. The emphasis on core content and skills in the 16–19 curriculum[5] has recently become another area for exploration and development.

This new role is a demanding one which requires a degree of collaboration for which teachers are often unprepared. Furthermore, the necessary organizational structures are rarely in existence. Reports of initiatives by individual Economics teachers and LEA groups recognize these constraints – nothing is achieved without a great deal of work, ingenuity and enthusiasm – but readers are left with a sense not of defeat but of success and possibilities for development.[6]

Some schools, as a result of economic awareness initiatives, have begun to identify problems and management issues involved in exploring the implications of cross-curricular activities for coherence and collaboration. Two areas of concern are apparent. The first arises because of the perceived need in some schools for all teachers to gain expertise in contexts described as 'economic' so as to safeguard the development of their own economic awareness. The second area of concern arises from the need to secure the coherence of pupils' whole-curriculum experiences.

Both require schools to conduct curriculum audits so that teachers can identify economic contexts in their own work and know what tasks their pupils are likely to be given in other curriculum subjects. But curriculum audits of this kind do not guarantee that the experiences gained by students will be coherent. Our current work in schools, reported in *Economic Awareness* and in LEA publications (see Note 2) indicates that progress can be made both towards achieving coherence and helping teachers to gain expertise if teachers of different subjects are enabled to meet each other in order to examine similarities and differences in the ways they help pupils to explore economic/

social/political/environmental issues arising from their subject work. Only if school managers are made aware of the possibilities are they in a position to respond as they review their use of resources to deliver the National Curriculum. The role of the Economics teacher in raising the awareness of school managers and in drawing their attention to the experiences of others is crucial.

Notes

1. The Economics Association's quarterly journal, *Economics* and the third edition of *Teaching Economics*, published by Heinemann Educational Books, contain accounts of most of the significant work in the field.
2. A considerable literature exists. Approximately 50 of the 80 or so LEAs with whom EcATT has worked have produced their own materials in the form of reports of classroom and review activities. These are listed in the January 1991 edition, (number 8) of EcATT's Newsletter, published by Longman and available from EcATT, University of London, Institute of Education, 20, Bedford Way, London, WC1H OAL. *Economic Awareness*, the termly journal, published by Longman, contains similar accounts. The BBC's Economic Awareness INSET programmes provide illustrations, on video, of both classrooms and the process of review.
3. This format was adopted in the legislation for Economic Awareness in Northern Ireland.
4. This format was adopted in the report of the Welsh Task Group, *Economic and Industrial Understanding: A Pupil Entitlement in the National Curriculum in Wales*, published by TVEI in 1989.
5. See, for example, the following:
    NCC (1990) *Core Skills 16–19: A Response to the Secretary of State*. National Curriculum Council, York.
    DES (1981) *Post-16 Education and Training: Core Skills, an HMI Paper*. HMSO, London.
    NCVQ (1990) *R & D Report No. 6 Common Learning Outcomes: Core Skills in A/AS levels and NVQs*. NCVQ, London.
    SEAC (1990) *Consultation on the Draft Principles for GCE Advanced Supplementary and Advanced Examinations*. SEAC, London.
6. Videos of Economic Awareness classroom and teacher group work have been produced by teachers of economics in Surrey LEA and by teachers of economics and others in the Wiltshire TVEI Swindon cluster in conjunction with EcATT. Details are available from EcATT (see note 2).

References

BBC (1988) 'Notes for teachers and course leaders in support of two television programmes in the BBC's Teacher Education Project on Economic Awareness'. BBC Education, London.

DES (1988) *Mathematics Working Group Report*, August. DES.

DES (1988) *Science Working Group Report*, August. DES.

DES (1989) *English for Ages 5–16 Working Group Report*, June. DES.

DES (1989) *English in the National Curriculum*, p. 34. HMSO.

DES (1989) *Mathematics in the National Curriculum*, p. 25 AT9. HMSO.

DES (1989) *Science in the National Curriculum*, AT13. HMSO.

DES (1989) *Science in the National Curriculum*, p. 29 AT13. HMSO.

DES (1990) *History Working Group Final Report*, April. DES.

Hodkinson, S and Thomas, L (1989) 'Balancing Act', *The Times Educational Supplement*, 2 October.

NCC (1989) *Circular 6: The National Curriculum and Whole Curriculum Planning Preliminary Guidance*. National Curriculum Council, York.

Thomas, L. and Hodkinson, S. (1988) 'What is Economic Awareness?' *Economic Awareness*, 1, 1.

6 How Local Education Authorities might Develop Economics Education

David Butler

The current state of play

The history of Economics education in schools differs from that of most other subjects in that it was first established as a strong A level subject and only in comparatively recent times has its importance in the pre-16 curriculum been fully recognized. This historical background has important and perhaps unique implications for the present and future development of Economics education in LEAs. It has had to fight hard for a place in the 'new curriculum' of the 1990s. Educators have needed to work out the types of Economics education suitable for younger pupils without any substantial information base. The notion of Economics education as an entitlement for all pupils will place great demands upon the in-service training of teachers.

Economics remains important at A level. It is now the third largest subject entry, and it looks like maintaining its market share. There does not seem to have been a loss of candidates to Business Studies, despite the very considerable recent growth in entries in this subject. Economics is also important in further education, in non-A level courses such as in CPVE and BTEC courses.

Below the Sixth Form and Further Education, the picture is far less clear. There are substantial entries in GCSE Economics, but many of these are from post-16 candidates. An important development, however, has been the growth of broad based Business Studies courses, which have often been introduced to replace subjects like Commerce, and skills courses such as typing and office practice. These Business Studies courses often contain a substantial Economics input. The distinction between Economics and Business Studies is increasingly blurred. Indeed, many schools and LEAs would regard them both as a subset of business education. Appointments to advisory and inspection services are increasingly being made for business education, a term which spans the fields of Economics and Business Studies. A similar view is taken by a recent Training Agency publication which regards business education as developing an understanding of both business and economic issues (TVEI, 1990).

During the 1980s, the notion of economic awareness/understanding as part of the pre-16 entitlement gained increasing acceptance. The publication of the NCC's *Curriculum Guidance 4, Educating for Economic and Industrial Understanding* (NCC, 1990) has given this further impetus, although debate continues as to what is appropriate economic education for 5–16 year olds. The school picture is patchy. There is much work of interest in both primary schools and secondary schools. Attempts have been made to deliver economic understanding through curriculum slots, Personal and Social Education programmes and as a cross-curricular theme through core and foundation subjects. The indications from inspection reports, however, tend to show an inconsistent provision within schools, between schools and between LEAs. The publication of the statutory orders for technology, which include substantive elements of economic and business education, has again given a new focus to work in this area and LEAs and schools are beginning to address the ways in which these aspects are best delivered.

What are we trying to achieve?

What sort of economics education should LEAs provide in the 1990s?

It has already been suggested that Economics is increasingly being seen as part of business education, and this is the view adopted in this and subsequent sections. Guidelines for Economics should not be seen in isolation from those for the broader area of business education.

The primary years (key stages 1 and 2)

There would appear to be two main thrusts to Economics education in the primary years. First, economic and industrial understanding needs to be considered as a cross-curricular theme. Second, National Curriculum Technology places legal obligations on schools to teach certain economic and business ideas to all pupils.

Economic understanding is likely to be developed through the existing curriculum in core and foundation subjects, where these are taught separately, and through topic work covering a range of other subjects. Experience suggests that primary teachers are able, with the right assistance, to incorporate economic perspectives into their existing schemes of work without adding further to an already overcrowded curriculum. There is a growing body of case studies illustrating work in economic understanding in primary schools (Economics Association, 1989; Longman, 1991; Ross, 1990). *Curriculum Guidance 4* also provides some useful examples of primary practice and suggests the types of knowledge, understanding, skills and attitudes that might be appropriate at this level.

Local Authority advisers and inspectors should be looking for evidence in primary schools of pupils being given opportunities to discuss, review and develop economic perspectives where they naturally occur. The current indications are that there are plenty of contexts in which to develop economic understanding, but the potential is often not fully exploited. There is sometimes a tendency for teachers to impose their own value positions rather than using the contexts to open up the discussion of economic issues.

Many primary schools have developed links with local firms and other commercial organizations. Many use various forms of enterprise education as a way of delivering aspects of the National Curriculum. These would seem to offer very useful contexts for developing economic understanding. At the same time, there is often a misunderstanding that these in themselves are sufficient to ensure that pupils are engaged in the development of economic understanding. There should be evidence that pupils are given the opportunity to question and review their experiences, if real economic understanding is to be achieved.

Technology would appear to be particularly important in developing economics education in the primary school. Early evidence tends to indicate that the economic aspects of technology projects are relatively weak. Where they are dealt with, the teacher often adopts too narrow a view, regarding a simple costings exercise as the 'economics' of the project.

The secondary curriculum

The secondary school will need to address the same issues with regard to Economics education as the primary school, but these issues are made more complex by the subject orientated nature of the secondary curriculum. A whole school approach to economic and industrial understanding becomes more difficult with the need for coordination across perhaps ten subject areas. An holistic approach to technology which incorporates economics and business education becomes harder when several disciplines are involved.

Economic and industrial understanding

Secondary schools may find it useful to carry out a curriculum audit in order to ascertain the extent to which the various subjects contribute to the development of economic and industrial understanding. These are, however, inherent dangers and shortcomings involved in curriculum audits. There needs to be a shared view of what economic and industrial understanding is. There is a tendency for teachers to identify subject content rather than processes as being 'economics' – 'we cover the Great Crash in history', 'we deal with energy conservation in science', 'we use economic statistics in mathematics'. What needs to be considered is *how* teachers use these contexts to develop economic understanding. Are they being used to explore economic ideas? Are pupils given the opportunity to question and challenge 'economic' statements and to reflect on the experiences gained from the contexts? As in the primary school, there needs to be classroom evidence of economic understanding in order to support curriculum statements. Advisers and inspectors clearly have a key role in trying to identify this evidence.

The indications are that economic understanding has little chance of success as a cross-curricular theme in secondary schools unless there is a coordinator, a well structured programme of INSET, and the support of senior management.

Technology

Technology at key stage 3 involves sophisticated economic and business ideas. Early evidence indicates that problems are being experienced in successfully implementing these aspects of Technology. Where specialist Economics and business education teachers are available in the school, it is important that they are involved in the planning of Technology projects. Their commitments at key stage 4 and beyond may well prevent them from being involved in the actual teaching of Technology in the lower school but they should be able to advise on how economic ideas and issues can be explored through Technology projects. Economics has a key role to play in the identification of needs and the evaluation of systems, artefacts and environments.

There are particular problems for the Economics teachers in Technology, even when they are available on the timetable. Most secondary schools are a long way from having multi-skilled Technology teachers, and some do not even see this as desirable. Because specialisms are likely to be retained, the role of Economics teachers needs to be given careful consideration. The other subjects which make up Technology often involve working with materials and the development of specific skills. Economics is mainly about ways of thinking. There will often be physical areas allocated to food, art and craft. What will pupils expect in the economics and business area? It might be argued that there should not be a separate economics/business area, but that the teachers will need to service all the other areas.

Specialist options

The indications are that there will be a great deal more flexibility at key stage 4 than was first envisaged when the proposals for the National Curriculum were published. It now seems likely that there will be curriculum space for Economics and Business Studies. Specific criteria for GCSE Economics and Business Studies are being prepared which will take account of the National Curriculum, particularly Technology.

Broad-based Business Studies courses and Economics should be available to pupils who wish to develop more specialized knowledge. There are exciting and interesting possibilities, with pupils being given the opportunity to link economic and business education with technology, modern languages and enterprise education.

Post-16 education

In post-16 education, it is likely that economic and industrial understanding will continue to be a cross-curricular theme. Where appropriate, A and A/S courses will make reference to economic issues. Post-16 TVEI in most LEAs again gives strong support to business education and the work-related curriculum. As with the lower school, there will again be important implications for INSET and for the assessment of this work. Recent HMI reports have highlighted the apparent lack of progression in work in this area, and schools and other institutions will need to address this complex issue.

Many pupils will wish to take specialized courses in business education, in

A level Economics and Business Studies and in BTEC courses. As with GCSE, there is a growing number of exciting possibilities of linking business education with foreign languages and Information Technology. Modular courses will further extend the range of combinations. It is also likely that pupils will be able to make 'credit transfers' between A level and NVQ courses. New courses are also increasingly blurring the distinction between Economics and Business Studies.

The work-related curriculum

Work experience and enterprise education are increasingly becoming an entitlement, particularly where TVEI has influenced the curriculum. There are clear links with Economics education. Economics can help pupils make greater sense of their experiences in these areas. The experiences gained through enterprise education and work experience can also help pupils to develop their economic understanding. Recent HMI reports, however, indicate that these links are often missing (HMI, 1990). Teachers of business education will need to pay careful attention to the relationships between their subjects and the work related curriculum.

How do we get there?

Force field analysis in education suggests that the adviser needs to identify the forces for and against change and then to enhance the positive factors and weaken the negative ones. It is perhaps useful at this stage to summarize some of the factors working for and against the current development of business education.

The negatives

- Business education is not a National Curriculum core or foundation subject.
- There is a lack of suitably trained teachers.
- There is a lack of advisory support in many LEAs.
- The development of economic and industrial understanding as a cross-curricular theme places very considerable demands upon INSET.
- Many business education teachers are fully committed at key stage 4 and beyond and do not have the time to share their expertise in the lower-school curriculum.
- There is a particular lack of support and available expertise to develop business education in the primary school.

The positives

- The Education Reform Act makes it clear that schools should demonstrate that their curricula are relevant and prepare young people for adult life. Business education would appear to have a key role to play in achieving this.

- Economic and industrial understanding is identified by the NCC as a cross-curricular theme in both pre-16 and post-16 education.
- There is a substantial amount of business education contained in Technology, and increasingly, National Curriculum core and foundation subjects, GCSE and A level, are addressing economic issues.
- Business education is strongly supported by TVEI.
- Business education is a very popular choice post-16.
- There is often strong support for business education from industrial governors, elected members and parents.

Strategies for getting there

An LEA policy for business education

It will be important for LEAs to have clear curriculum statements on business education. Such statements need to adopt an holistic approach to economic and industrial understanding, business studies, industry links and enterprise education. They need to be cross referenced with other curriculum statements, particularly with technology. Appropriate levels of resourcing need to be specified, together with the mechanisms for the delivery of the policy. The statements need to be shared with and have the support of teachers, heads, advisers, inspectors and elected members.

The policy statement needs to be translated into a working document. One approach is to develop an *aide memoire* or a set of performance indicators which can be used by teachers, heads, advisers and inspectors to evaluate business education provision in schools. It is important for teachers to be fully involved in the development of such a document. One such attempt is included in Appendix 6.1.

Schools will be able to use the LEA policy statement and the *aide memoire* to produce their own whole-school policy and development plan for business education. They should be encouraged to produce their own set of performance indicators which is agreed with the appropriate inspector. They will then be able to carry out a self-review of business education provision.

Advisory support

A considerable number of LEAs are without specialist advisers or inspectors for business education. There is clear evidence that LEAs in this position tend to lag behind national developments in business education, and the quality of teaching and learning is often lower. As the share of the budget held centrally by LEAs is reduced, it will be crucially important for teachers to lobby the education committee for advisory support in business education.

Even in large education authorities, it is rare to find more than one adviser, although there may be additional support from advisory teachers. It is clear that the adviser needs to work through a range of networks and seek the support of external agencies.

It is important that the adviser for business education works with advisory colleagues and inspectors. Advisory colleagues will need to have a clear grasp of economic and industrial understanding if it is to be successfully developed in primary schools and as a cross-curricular theme in secondary schools.

Many LEAs, often with the help of outside funding, have been able to appoint a variety of advisory staff to support school–industry work. Many are also in the process of establishing education–business partnerships with the Training and Enterprise Councils. Business education has an important role to play within these networks in helping to establish a clear rationale for their work. They are also of major value in helping to deliver the business education curriculum.

Increasingly, LEAs are measuring the cost effectiveness of their advisory services, and school, under local financial management, have the power to buy in services from outside the LEA. A close working relationship with some of these external agencies will be important and often mutually beneficial. Links with teacher training organizations provide an example of this. They may be able to provide cost effective INSET and retraining programmes, particularly where they span a number of small LEAs. Such links may also help to provide a supply of newly trained teachers of business education if the LEA can offer teaching practice placements.

Many LEAs have formed a working partnership with the Economics Association. The Association is increasingly concerning itself with broad based business education, and has a network of local branches which support teachers of Economics and Business Studies. Many local branches organize INSET activities and conferences for students. In return, the LEA might provide free advertising and possibly travel costs for teachers attending meetings.

In addition to these networks, the adviser may well find it useful to establish local support groups. TVEI has also encouraged local consortia which attract varying degrees of financial support. They are often self-supporting groups, which again provide a network which the adviser can use to disseminate information, new developments and ideas.

Finally, effective lines of communication to teachers and between teachers is of key importance in supporting business education. Many LEAs have their own business education newsheets, and increasing use is being made of electronic mail systems.

Conclusions and crystal ball gazing

Much has happened in Economics education in the 1980s. It has made a substantial impact on the years of compulsory education whilst remaining immensely strong in post-16 education. It is being increasingly accepted as part of the 5–18 entitlement curriculum.

The 1990s will see coherence developing in all aspects of education, and economics will not be an exception. It is argued in this chapter that the likely route of this coherence in many LEAs will be through its absorption into a framework of broad based business education which includes economic and industrial understanding, aspects of the work related curriculum and technology as well as specialist courses in economics and business studies.

Appendix 6.1

Aide memoire/ performance indicators for economics and business education (Summary developed from work by Kent teachers, July 1990)

Management

- Is there a whole school policy/development plan for Economics/business education? (Who was involved in its construction? How often is it reviewed?)
- How does the departmental policy document relate to the whole-school development plan? How does it interrelate with other policy statements, eg Technology?
- Is economic and industrial understanding an entitlement for all pupils? (How has the school responded to *Curriculum Guidance 4*? Is Economic and Industrial Understanding being addressed across the curriculum?)
- How are the economics/business aspects of National Curriculum Technology being delivered?
- Are there broad based business education courses or Economics courses available as options at GCSE (and Sixth Form level)? (Are they available to all ability levels? What percentage of the year group opt for these courses?)
- What is the senior management view of Economics/business education?
- Are there regular departmental meetings? Is there a flow of information between the department and senior management?
- What are the timetabling arrangements for Economics/business education – are there appropriate blocks of time?

Resourcing

- Is there an adequate and qualified number of staff available to deliver the Economics/business education curriculum?
- What share of capitation does Economics/business education receive?
- Do students in Economics/business education have reasonable access to IT?
- Are there specialist rooms for Economics/business education? (How does the location of these rooms relate to other relevant areas?)
- Are there display board facilities?
- Are there adequate duplicating facilities available to the department?
- What is the provision of up-to-date texts, software, learning resources?
- How are learning resources organized? How accessible are they to the pupils?
- What use is made of the wider community? (eg, visits, use of AOTs).
- What INSET is the department involved in? (Is there a developmental programme? What recognizable difference has it made?)

The quality of the learning experience

- Is there a range and balance of teaching/learning styles? (Didactic, active, investigative, individual, group, simulations, case studies, etc.)
- Are pupils encouraged to take responsibility for their own learning?
- Are pupils clear about the objectives of the work they are engaged in?
- Are learning activities designed to allow for the full ability range?
- Is there evidence of progression in the work being undertaken?
- How are pupil achievements celebrated? (Displays of work?)
- What is the quality of teacher/pupil and pupil/pupil relationships?
- Are pupils being motivated by the activities? (Are they keen to 'get on' with the next task, keen to discuss their work etc?)
- What use is made of outside agencies?
- How is work experience being used by the Economics/business education department?
- What use is being made of IT?
- In subjects other than Economics/business education, are pupils being encouraged to question and challenge 'economic statements'? Can pupils apply their economic understanding in a variety of contexts?
- Are there opportunities for teachers to work together both within the department and with teachers from other departments? (Are teachers given the opportunity to review their work with colleagues?)

Assessment

- Is there a departmental policy on assessment? (How does it relate to the whole-school policy on assessment and records of achievement?)
- Are pupils involved in their own assessment?
- Is there a dialogue on assessment between teacher and pupil?
- Are a range of assessment procedures employed?
- Is there a commonly agreed system of marking? (Is it criterion-referenced? Is it designed to reward positive achievement?)
- How is work moderated within the department?
- How are the results of assessment recorded?
- Is the assessment scheme designed to help pupils set future targets?
- What are pupil achievements in public examinations? (In relation to intake ability, in relation to other departments, in relation to county/national averages?)

References

Economics Association (1989) *Primary Economic Awareness Pack*, Economics Association Haywards Heath.

HMI (1990) *Report on Work Experience in Schools and Enterprise Education in Schools* HMSO, London.

Longman (1991) *Economic Awareness Guides*. Longman, Harlow.

NCC (1990) *Curriculum Guidance 4. Educating for Economic and Industrial Understanding*. National Curriculum Council, York.

Ross, A (ed.) (1990) *Economic and Industrial Awareness in the Primary School*. Polytechnic of North London Press and School Curriculum Industry Partnership, London.

TVEI (1990) *Business Education. A Handbook for Schools*. Training Agency, Sheffield.

7 Testing Economics Understanding

William B. Walstad

Introduction

Problem-solving or decision-making lies at the heart of Economics. The discipline developed from the need to solve the economics problems facing individuals and societies. The condition of scarcity means that productive resources are limited relative to people's wants. Consequently, a choice must be made about how to use limited resources in the most efficient way possible to satisfy those unlimited wants. Scarcity gives rise to the study of Economics and its application to all decisions.

Certainly an Economics course requires the teacher to make decisions. Perhaps the most difficult one involves the selection of the type of classroom test that will be used for assessing student achievement in Economics. The possibilities are varied, and usually include essay or multiple choice, to name the more common types. The problem for the teacher is to decide how to select the type that will best achieve the instructional goals, given that resources (classroom and student time) are limited.

Economics decision-making

This situation requires the use of Economics decision-making in much the same way that it is taught to students in Economics courses. There are five familiar steps to follow in the basic model:

(1) define the problem;
(2) specify the alternatives;
(3) state the criteria;
(4) evaluate the alternatives; and,
(5) make a decision.

In this case, the first step should be clear: the teacher must decide what form of classroom testing will be used to measure student achievement in Economics. All the other steps deserve more elaboration.

Specifying alternatives

The specification of alternative measures of understanding in Economics can be tedious, because there are so many forms of pencil-and-paper tests. In general, most test types can be classified into two categories. *Constructed-response* tests require that the student construct a response to an item or series of items by writing, by calculating, or by graphing. The constructed-response category would include essays, short-answer (ie definitions or brief questions), and numerical or word problems. With the exception of the longer essay question, constructed-response items are completed by students in a short amount of time, anywhere from 1 to 15 minutes. In contrast, *fixed-response* items ask the student to select the best answer from a fixed set of answers. Multiple choice, true–false, and classification items are the more popular types of fixed-response items. Table 7.1 presents examples of constructed- and fixed-response items.

Criteria

The third step in Economics decision-making involves stating the criteria. In the test-type decision, the criteria would be a listing of what the teacher thinks is important in choosing a test format. The possible criteria for selecting the type of classroom test to administer to students are many. Teachers sometimes prefer tests that are *easy to construct* or that are *easy to score*. A measure might be desired because it can include many questions to *cover the test domain*. Another factor to consider is the *potential for bias in scoring* because of the subjective nature of grading items. Some test types are preferred because of the *freedom of response* for the student to write answers to questions or to express opinions. Opportunities for *guessing* or *bluffing* are factors that are occasionally taken into account when considering a test type. Finally, a teacher may be concerned with how a test measures the student learning in higher levels of the *cognitive domain*.[1]

Evaluating alternatives

Once the major criteria or objectives are clearly stated, the teacher has a basis for conducting an evaluation of each test alternative. A decision matrix with the objectives listed across the top and the alternatives listed down the left side might be useful in the evaluation; such a matrix is shown in Table 7.2

The matrix gives teachers an overall picture of both the range of alternatives and the important factors to consider in making the choice. Each alternative is then judged in terms of how well it meets each criterion. This judgement can be made in words, with the main descriptors written in each box, or a numerical score can be assigned to each box based on a rating scale. A simple rating system would give a project a +1 or +2 depending on the degree to which it meets a criterion. A −1 or −2 would be assigned depending on the extent to which an alternative works against a criterion. If there is uncertainty

Constructed-response items

Essay: 'I don't know much about the tariff. I do know that when I buy a coat from England, I have the coat and England has the money. But when I buy a coat in America, I have the coat and America has the money'. (Attributed to Abraham Lincoln).

Do you agree with Mr. Lincoln? Analyse the economic case for or the economic case against a tariff on coats.

Short-answer: In some industries, producers justify their reluctance to lower prices by arguing that the demand for their products is inelastic. Briefly explain.

Problem: In a hypothetical economy in Year 1, nominal GNP was 3774 billion pounds and the price index was 108. In Year 2, nominal GNP was 3989 billion pounds and the price index was 112. What was real GNP in Year 1 and Year 2? What was the percentage increase in real GNP from Year 1 to Year 2?

Fixed-response

Multiple Choice: An increase in the US dollar price of British pounds will:

A. increase the pound price of dollars.
B. decrease the pound price of dollars.
C. leave the pound price of dollars unchanged.
D. cause Britain's terms of trade with the US to deteriorate.

True–False: True False: If the slope of the linear relationship between consumption and income was .90, then it tells us that for every 1 pound increase in income, there will be a .90 pound increase in consumption.

Classification: Below is a list of economic statements. Label each as to whether they are positive (P) or normative (N).

New York City should control the rental price of apartments.

Consumer price rose at an annual rate of 5 per cent last year.

Most people who are unemployed are just too lazy to work.

Generally speaking, if you lower the price of a product, people will buy more of the product.

Table 7.1 *Examples of constructed- and fixed-response items*
Source: R Bingham and W B Walstad, 1990.

in the evaluation, the ± sign would be attached to an evaluation. A zero (0) would be entered into the matrix if the alternative is not related to a criterion.

Table 7.2 shows the results of a simple evaluation of the alternatives against the criteria, assuming that each criterion receives an equal weight.

The essay and short-answer format have a total score of 0, which is the highest score when ratings are summed across criteria. The multiple choice ranking would come next, with a score of −1. Problems and true–false items have a total score of −2. Classification items received the lowest rating of −3. Under this rating system, the results would suggest that essays or short answer questions are the best to use.

Weighting the criteria: essays or multiple choice?

To make matters more complex, but more realistic, each criterion should be weighted to reflect the relative importance of a particular criterion for teachers. Different weights can substantially change the results of the total score and make a strong case for selecting one testing format rather than another.

Multiple choice tests, for example, can be shown to have distinct advantages over the more appealing alternatives, the essay test, and its short-answer derivative, based on the weights assigned to the test selection criteria. The most compelling advantage arises from the constraints facing teachers. When class sizes are large, it is very time-consuming to mark essays and more difficult to give quick feedback to students. Spending hours reading essays means less time available for other teaching duties. The marking time for multiple choice tests is negligible, so that if *economy in scoring* were given double weight in the matrix, then the overall score for the multiple choice format would increase to +1 and the essay rating would drop to −2.

Some instructors think that the economy in scoring offered by multiple choice tests cheapens the education of students. Personal preference aside, there is no evidence to suggest that multiple choice tests are less effective ways to measure student achievement in Economics. In fact, multiple choice tests provide a more objective assessment of Economics understanding because there is *no bias in grading*. Bias in essay scoring comes from such factors as knowing the name of the student, the mood of the teacher, the order in which essays are read, how many times the essays are read, and the importance given to matters of composition. None of these sources of bias enter the scoring of multiple choice tests. Also, multiple-choice questions are highly structured, with one correct answer, and contain none of the vagueness that affects the marking of essays.

Another benefit comes from the ability to *sample the content domain*. Essay tests with three questions, or short-answer tests with five to seven questions, may assess only a limited portion of the content domain of an Economics course. Multiple choice tests, in contrast, usually contain 30–40 questions, and allow the teacher more flexibility in evaluating students on a much wider range of content. The teacher can also measure the depth of understanding by placing a series of questions on the same topic in the exam.

The advantages of less bias and wider sampling of the content domain mean that multiple choice tests are more reliable indicators of student performance than essay tests.[2] With essays, there is a much stronger element of chance influencing the test score, because students may be unlucky when the teacher asks one of three essay questions on a topic that the student did not study; it is less likely that one-third of the multiple choice questions will be on material that the student did not study. The measurement error introduced from the subjective nature of marking compounds the problem. When the coverage and bias factors are given a double weight, the rating for the multiple choice format jumps by two points to +3 while the essay score drops to −4.

The availability of test banks for multiple-choice questions in economics also means that the time required to set tests that match the course content is considerably reduced.[3] Test banks may change the rating given to *ease of test construction* in Table 7.2. It used to be the rule that essay tests took less time to prepare (+1) but more time to mark, while multiple choice tests took substantially more time to prepare (−2) and less time to mark. With published test banks, the rating for ease of construction for multiple choice tests might be revised to +1, which would increase the overall score for the multiple choice format to +6.

Cognitive level

Teachers often believe that multiple choice questions operate at the lower cognitive levels, while essays are thought to assess higher-order thinking in students; hence the +2 rating for essays and the −1 rating for multiple choice.[4] This argument really depends on the quality of each test, and it is not a given feature of each test format. Many multiple choice items can be written to assess student understanding at higher cognitive levels. Consider the following stimuli and question:

	Rice	*Wheat*
Country A	20	40
Country B	15	60

The table above shows points from straight-line production possibilities schedules for country A and country B. If the two countries engage in trade, the terms of trade will most likely be between:

A. 1 and 2 units of wheat for 1 unit of rice.
B. 2 and 4 units of wheat for 1 unit of rice.
C. 3 and 5 units of rice for 1 unit of wheat.
D. ½ and ¾ units of rice for 1 unit of wheat.

This analytical question requires the student to interpret production possibilities data, calculate opportunity costs for each country to determine the comparative advantage, and to select the likely terms of trade between the nations.

Essay tests may not always demonstrate that students show complex understanding. Asking students to 'explain why most modern industrial nations have a central bank' (eg, US Federal Reserve System) may not reveal higher-level thinking, because the students will probably 'regurgitate' the five reasons a teacher gave in a lesson or that were listed in the textbook. Essays also can be so vague and unstructured that there might be several possibilities for student response. An essay question such as 'criticize minimum wage laws' may produce

Criteria

Alternatives	Ease of test construction	Economy in scoring	Coverage of test domain	Potential for bias in scoring	Freedom of response/ writing	Opportunity for guessing/ bluffing	Tap higher cognitive levels	Total score
Essay	Few items, hard to write +1	Difficult, much time -2	Narrow, few items -1	Yes -1	Yes, great +2	Yes -1	Higher, all +2	0
Short-answer	Few items, easy to write +2	Relatively easy, some time -1	Narrow, few items -1	Yes -1	Yes, some +1	Yes -1	Higher, limited +1	0
Problems (Verbal or Numerical)	Few items, hard to write +1	Relatively easy, some time -1	Narrow, few items -1	Yes -1	No -1	No +1	Yes, limited +1	-1
Multiple Choice	Many items, hard to write -2	Very easy, little time +2	Very wide (many items and flexible) +1	No +1	No -1	Yes -1	Varies, mostly lower -1	-1
True-False	Many items, easy to write -1	Very easy, little time +2	Very wide (many items and flexible) +1	No +1	No -1	Yes, great -2	Lower -2	-2
Classification	Many items, easy to write -1	Very easy, little time +2	Limited format for some content -1	No +1	No -1	Yes -1	Lower -2	-3

Table 7.2 Evaluating testing formats

several responses that are valid from an economics perspective, but do not necessarily require the student to use the supply and demand analysis that the instructor wanted students to use in explaining the problems with an increase in the minimum wage. Several well-written items in choice format could handle either the central bank or the minimum wage topic at several cognitive levels with more precision and in less time for the student to answer and the teacher to mark.

Making a decision and other factors

The point of the discussion is not to persuade Economics teachers to use multiple choice tests and to abandon essays, because a strong case can also be made for the use of the essay (Welsh and Saunders, 1990). Nor is the point to show how to assign a precise rating to each test type. The recommendation for teachers is to give more attention to the *purpose* of the classroom assessment. If the purpose is to find out what students know and whether they can apply basic concepts to new situations, then fixed-response tests can handle that objective quite well in many cases and are sometimes preferred to constructed-response tests. If the purpose is to get students to express economics ideas through writing within time limits, then constructed-response items, such as the essay or short-answer questions, can be very useful to both the teacher and the student. If the purpose is to use the test for self-assessment or class discussion, then all forms may be useful. What must be understood for good classroom testing in economics are the *advantages* and *disadvantages* of each method for assessing students in light of the instructional objectives.

There will undoubtedly be trade-offs among the criteria in the final decision. For example, one of the major advantages of the verbal or numerical problem is that there is no opportunity for guessing or bluffing, as there is with essay, multiple choice, and true-false items. If the material the teacher covers is primarily quantitative, then numerical problems might be the best ones to use to assess students, to eliminate any doubts about student mastery of the quantitative content, despite the disadvantages of that type of item. Similarly, matching or classification exercises might prove to be useful for students trying to master understanding of terms or trying to distinguish differences.

Most testing types can also be modified to address important criteria. One of the great disadvantages of the true-false item is that there is a great chance of guessing the correct answer. This deficiency can be overcome, if the student is asked to give a brief statement about *why* they selected the true or the false response. Some creativity on the part of the teacher can make classroom assessment more fun and varied, whether the test is being used for diagnostic reasons, for drill and practice, or for giving marks. The conclusion is that there are many good types of test to use with students, depending on the purpose of the assessment.

Beyond the classroom test

Some teachers may wish to go beyond the classroom test and occasionally use a standardized achievement test in Economics. There are several reasons for this suggestion. Items for standardized measures are more carefully written than teacher-made items; they are also pre-tested and evaluated by a committee of economics experts. Unlike teacher-made tests, standardized tests provide a detailed manual, with information on test reliability, validity, and administration. Of most interest for classroom teachers, however, are the national norms. With a standardized test, teachers can administer the test to students and then compare the student or class scores to the performance of a representative national sample of students and across various student characteristics. These comparisons are not possible with a classroom test.

One example of a standardized test in economics available for teacher use is the *Test of Economic Literacy* (TEL) (Soper and Walstad, 1987). This multiple choice test contains 46 items on fundamental economic, microeconomic, macroeconomic, and international economics concepts that are written at various cognitive levels. Form A of this two-form test was originally developed in 1986 and nationally normed in the United States with 4235 students. In 1989, it was slightly modified and nationally normed with a representative sample of 7549 Sixth-Form students in the United Kingdom (Whitehead and Halil, 1989). Studies in both countries show TEL to be a reliable and valid measure of the general economics understanding for students in the 16–18 age range (Walstad and Soper, 1991; Whitehead and Halil, 1990). By administering the TEL to students, teachers can convert the raw scores to a national percentile ranking. A raw score of 32 on TEL, for example, would place a Sixth-Form student with Economics instruction at the fifty-first percentile on the TEL.

Information about student performance or skill in Economics can be collected in formats other than a standardized exam or classroom test. Teachers may want to know more about student *writing* than demonstrated in the time limits imposed by an essay or short-answer question. There are many options for assessing student writing in Economics depending on the time available for the teacher and the students (Petr, 1990). Papers can be assigned to students to explore controversial economic issues (eg, do the Japanese engage in unfair trading practices with their trading partners?). Students can be given an in-class or out-of-class assignment to interpret the economic meaning of selected editorial cartoons, or to explain a chart, a graph, or a data table in the newspaper. The teacher can ask students to keep logs or journals about current events in economics that might eventually become the source of information for a short paper. These are just a few of the possibilities for student writing.

Being able to *speak* intelligently about Economics is as important as being about to write about it. In fact, many activities that could be given as writing assignments should also be used to improve skill in the oral communication of Economics ideas. Oral reports can be assigned on various topics (eg, how will the United Kingdom be affected by monetary union with other European nations?). Case studies can be given to students to discuss in small groups and for later presentations to the whole class (eg, analyse the effects of OPEC oil price shocks on the world economy during the 1970s). Participation in simulations and the debriefing that follows can be used by the teacher to encourage class discussion and to obtain feedback on student understanding of Economic ideas (eg, Whitehead, 1988). In other words, the opportunities for developing oral communication skill in Economics are as unlimited as those for developing writing skills.

Although this chapter has focused primarily on the characteristics of traditional methods for classroom testing, these other activities should be encouraged, because they stimulate other dimensions of student learning and at the same time can be used for assessment purposes. By asking students to speak, to write, or to take a test on Economics, the teacher is asking the students to *think* about Economics and its application to issues and problems. The quality of the exams and complementary teaching activities will significantly influence the quality of the thinking about Economics that will occur in the classroom.

Notes

1. There are many other taxonomies of the cognitive domain. The most widely-used was outlined by Benjamin Bloom *et al.* (1956) and has six levels: (1) knowledge; (2) comprehension; (3) application; (4) analysis; (5) synthesis; and, (6) evaluation.
2. Reliability is measured on a scale from .00 to 1.00, with higher numbers indicating a more consistent measure. A study of college tests of English composition (Breland *et al.*, 1987) illustrates the difference: the reliability of single essays read once ranged from .36–.46, and only rose to the range of .53–.62 after being read three times; the reliability of the multiple choice tests were in the range of .84–.92. For a further discussion of the reliability and validity of standardized achievement tests in economics, see Walstad, 1987.
3. For a discussion of test banks, testing software, multiple choice testing, see Walstad (1990).
4. One study indicated that the cognitive level of multiple choice questions in test banks is often low. Karns, Burton, and Martin (1983) found in six principles of Economics textbooks that the large majority of the questions (70–90 per cent) were written at the knowledge and comprehension level of Bloom's taxonomy (see note 1).

References

Bingham, R and Walstad, W B (1990) *Study Guide to Accompany McConnell/Brue Economics.* McGraw-Hill, New York.

Bloom, B S, Englehart, M D, Furst, E J, Hill, W H and Krathwohl, D R (1956) *Taxonomy of Educational Objectives Handbook 1: Cognitive Domain.* David McKay, New York.

Breland, H, Camp, R, Jones, R J, Morris, M M and Rock, D (1987) *Assessing Writing Skill.* College Entrance Examination Board, New York.

Karns, J M L, Burton, G E, and Martin, G D (1983) 'Learning objectives and testing: An analysis of six principles of economics textbooks using Bloom's taxonomy', *Journal of Economic Education* 14, pp. 16–20.

Petr, J (1990) 'Student writing as a guide to student thinking', in Saunders, P, and Walstad W B (eds) *The Principles of Economics Course: A Handbook for Instructors.* McGraw-Hill, New York (pp. 127–40).

Soper, J C, and Walstad, W B (1987) *Test of Economic Literacy: Examiner's Manual* (2nd edn). Joint Council on Economic Education, New York.

Walstad, W B (1987) 'Measurement instruments', in Becker, W E and Walstad, W B (eds) *Econometric Modelling in Economic Education Research*. Kluwer-Nijhoff, Boston (pp. 73–98).

Walstad, W B (1990) 'Multiple choice tests for principles of economics courses', in Saunders, P and Walstad, W B (eds) *The Principles of Economics Course: A Handbook for Instructors*. McGraw-Hill, New York (pp. 209–21).

Walstad, W B and Soper, J C (1991) 'Economic literacy in senior high schools', in Walstad, W B and Soper, J C (eds) *Effective Economic Education in the Schools*. National Education Association, Washington, DC.

Welsh, A and Saunders, P (1990) 'Essay questions and tests' in Saunders, D and Walstad, W B (eds) *The Principles of Economics Course: A Handbook for Instructors*. McGraw-Hill, New York (pp. 192–208).

Whitehead, D J (ed.) (1988) *Trade-Offs: Simulations and Role Plays for Economics*. Longman, London.

Whitehead, D J and Halil, T (1989) 'The test of economic literacy: Standardization in the UK', *Research Papers in Economics Education*. Institute of Education, University of London, London.

Whitehead, D J and Halil, T (1990) 'Economic literacy in the UK and the USA: An empirical analysis', *Economics* 26, pp. 33–8.

SECTION 2: BUSINESS EDUCATION

8 The Business Studies Curriculum at A Level

David Dyer

Introduction

The term 'Business Studies' still conjures up a variety of images – more than 20 years after the development of the first A level syllabus. The common image used to be a group of skills: typing and shorthand and perhaps some office practice. This kind of understanding can still be found, though in most instances typing has been replaced by information processing. Even though 1967 saw the development of a new advanced level, no attempt has been made to reach agreement as to the core of the subject. Indeed the firm intention of the three pioneer boards was to differentiate, so as to find a niche in a small but growing market. Added to this search for a distinct 'trade mark' were three issues which affected them all: *relevance, acceptability, integrity*.

If Business Studies is not *relevant*, it has no market. But relevant to whom? Does the subject seek to satisfy the needs and interests of those who take it, or is that relevance related more to the needs of ultimate users? Is the subject relevant because it is an intellectual discipline alongside other A levels, or is it vocational? Built into this debate, which raged fiercely for many years, is the inference that perhaps it is meant for less able students, and some schools offered it as a subject because that view prevailed. The first A level on the market was offered by Cambridge, and its objectives make it quite clear where the relevance lies:

> The course provides a bridge between educational needs and the needs of life after school. [It aims] to develop skills in the analysis and solution of problems, handling and interpretation of data, investigating and reporting. To develop a facility for self-expression, ability to present ideas in a logical and cogent way, to integrate ideas drawn from several sources. [To promote] . . . understanding of how individuals and organisations cope with constraints, conflict and uncertainty, knowledge and appreciation of the co-operation and inter-dependence which participation in society entails.[1]

There are further aims which expand upon this combination of intellectual, social and behaviourial skills firmly embedded in the objectives. The AEB syllabus makes it equally clear that '[It] is not intended to be vocational. It aims to make candidates think about business in a critical manner.'[2]

Both syllabuses focus upon the needs of students. They claim nothing that is unique except the context in which the objectives are pursued. There is, perhaps, a more forceful focus on problem solving and dealing with uncertainty than may be found elsewhere. If there are vocational advantages, they are a 'spin off' which is of great value but is not an underlying objective.

The search for *acceptability* is the fate of all new subjects which must seek a niche within the limited resources of post-16 timetables and claim to be a stepping stone to higher education. It is the eternal problem of all change that it rarely takes place smoothly.

'Is it acceptable for university entrance?' is probably the question I have been asked most often, and it is closely followed by 'yes, but is it a rigorous subject?' What saddens me about the questions is that those who ask them do so without careful study of the evidence available. Few now question the rigour of Business Studies; in fact they are wary of allowing students who will struggle with A level to embark upon it. Some still worry about outside users, but the only restriction which exists is that many universities do not respond well to students who offer both Business Studies and Economics. I consider this an advantage rather than a weakness, for an A level profile which contains both is much too narrow to be regarded as good education.

That change should have to struggle is no bad thing. The changes which are worthwhile will stand the test of time, and Business Studies has. Nevertheless, there are traces within the syllabuses of the struggle for acceptance. The Cambridge Syllabus in its initial form burdened itself with a paper called Business Mathematics, in the pursuit of 'rigour' and 'acceptability'. Whilst there is need for quantitative competence and understanding in a Business Studies course, there is no real 'Maths', and that initial over-emphasis has coloured thinking about the syllabus ever since. Business Studies is acceptable, and there is a very large number of students at polytechnics and at universities, as well as in other walks of life, to attest to it.

Integrity is the search for coherence and discipline. I recall the days when, as a careers master, I studied the courses in Business Studies being offered by universities and re-acted to them as 'like taking 10 different A levels in Accounting, Statistics, Economics . . . rather than an integrated degree course'. All those who have developed A level Business Studies courses have been aware of this danger and have striven to ensure they are integrated, that the assessment supports those who teach in an integrating way, and that the objectives of the syllabus stress it.

AEB

In syllabuses up to 1988, Section 6 concentrated on topics which drew ideas from across the syllabus and required integration, re-inforcing this in their assessment by a long compulsory essay on a wide ranging topic in Part A of Paper 2.

Now they have moved to a case study as the means of assessment, and the mark allocation is greater. They assert the importance of the integrative approach in their Introduction: 'To enable students to become familiar with the breadth and depth of business by a study of the integrated nature of business problems'. This is re-inforced by the words used in Section 6 and the teachers' guidance notes which accompany it.[3]

Cambridge

The integrated nature of the course is strongly emphasized, both in the introduction and in the structure of the course. That structure is based upon a decision-making format, with a focus on the skills the student will develop and use in the process. The assessment is through three components. In the first, quantitative understanding is not assessed for its own sake, but in the context of a business problem and the need to show critical understanding of the technique used in that context. The second paper is now a case study, and paper 3 is extensive coursework requiring investigation within an organization and a report written in problem-solving format.[4]

Oxford

This board emphasized its special focus by calling the course 'Industrial Studies' rather than Business Studies, and this difference is reflected throughout the syllabus and its assessment. But it is undoubtedly of the same 'family', and firmly stresses the integrative approach, though the division into specialist topic areas in paper 2 does tend to pull the other way to some extent. In the introduction to the notes for guidance, it is asserted that:

> There is an underlying concept of the wholeness of the subject which must be made explicit. The intellectual challenge . . . arises from the need to identify and understand the relationships between the parts which contribute to understanding the subject as a whole. If this concern for the whole picture is neglected, the parts can become artificially simple.[5]

More recent syllabuses

The growth of Business Studies has been reflected in many new courses, all presenting a variation on the theme but all insisting, in different ways, on the wholeness of the subject. For example, the focus of the Business and Information Studies A Level is a Business Plan through which many of the elements of the course are delivered.[6] Cambridge has developed a modular A level which in principle is discrete, offering study of 5 modules. In practice, the first module, being one third of the subject, is a 'core' which is both assessed in its own right and in the foundation for the later option modules. Additionally, one third of the assessment is a research assignment which is an investigative study.[7]

The core of the subject

Two points stand out in this discussion: first approaches to Business Studies commonly see the whole as more important than its parts, the latter being important in relation to each other rather than for themselves. In some cases this is emphasized by the adoption of a theme, such as decision making or the business plan. In all cases, it is reflected in the assessment. Second, there is emphasis on the skills that those who follow the course will develop, rather than upon the content they will follow.

Nevertheless, teachers need to know what they are to teach, and questions as to the breadth or depth in which a subject is to be studied are always asked. Answers can only be provided over time by the experience the teacher develops and the evidence gathered. The almost universal experience of the early years of teaching is that too much is taught too extensively, and that topics are taught in an isolated way which denies the strong push for integration already identified.

There is a further problem, universal in teaching but particularly relevant in the early years of teaching Business Studies. This is the perspective from which the subject is taught. Although a small number of teachers are initially trained in Business Studies, the majority of those teaching A level are doing so on the basis of in-service training or without specific training. The most common origin of such teachers is Economics or Sociology. Such teachers often find it difficult to adopt the perspective of their former discipline which is needed within Business Studies. The problem is sometimes further increased when other school specialists are called in to assist. The most common occurrence is the use of Maths teachers, whose approach is not contextual and is often too concerned with the techniques themselves. Life is made more difficult for many students when the language of mathematics is used to formulate or explain the technique being used. Students do have to use a range of tools to solve problems, they do have to understand when a technique is appropriate and they must be able to offer critical explanations of the contribution the technique makes to the solution of the problem. They do not have to have a mathematician's understanding of the technique or the processes.

The first real attempt to determine an agreed core for Business Studies was made in the development of the National Criteria for the subject at GCSE.[8] It will serve as a model for discussion. In the criteria, five compulsory areas of study are set out, although considerable freedom is given within them. They are:

> The environment within which business operates.
> The structure and organization of business.
> Business behaviour.
> People in business.
> Aiding and controlling business behaviour.

There is a perceptible logic to these topics, leading from the environment through the organization and structure of business to its behaviour, finally considering the way interests outside business need to be involved in its behaviour. Logic might suggest that 'people' should be considered before 'behaviour' since it is through people that such behaviour must take place. Many readers might be happy with that framework, but it can be further divided into two elements, those which are concerned with the dynamics of business and those (1 and 5) which relate to the environment of business.

Several syllabuses have a common core. Two of these are generally available and we can use them to test the validity of this framework.

Common core in Industrial Studies[5]

The common core of the syllabus is examined in Paper 1, which is divided into two sections. To enable teachers to work to this pattern, the syllabus is also divided in like manner. This makes it a little difficult to identify the elements of our model within the course, but it is clear that they are there.

The environment

Mostly treated in 1(a) and with a firm economic flavour. It is stressed that the topic is more a foundation and a frame of reference than an object of detailed study. In 1(f) an international perspective is added, and 2(a) widens an otherwise narrowly economic perspective into a consideration of attitudes towards industry and industry in society (2[b]).

Business organization

1(b) looks specifically at the financing of industry and in (iii) sets the framework for problem solving about the raising of finance. B(1) is a comprehensive examination of the need for and nature of organization. It stresses the need to study both the concepts and structures of organizations and the way that organization is managed. There is little here that we would not expect to see in a Business Studies syllabus, and nothing we might want to see is missed out. Some might argue that the content is heavy and assumes too great an importance as compared with the skills being sought.

Business behaviour

There are three elements of this: Marketing, Production and Accounting. The special feature of this syllabus is that it goes well beyond the core in relation to the Production function and the technology of it. Market orientation is clearly established in 1(d). The functional elements of marketing are part of 2(b), but it is made clear that the core is only concerned with what a marketing department does and not how it is done. Here the existence of a 'Marketing' option clearly limits what is done in the core. The accounting elements come in the costing involved in production and in section 5(a) dealing with measurement of performance and 5(b) looking at profit. All the areas of business behaviour envisaged by the framework receive some treatment, but the balance and focus, particularly in the treatment of marketing, is not typical.

People in business

1(c) considers labour and wages from the viewpoint of the economist. In B(4), the approach usually associated with Business Studies is adopted. There is a human relations option, and this perhaps explains the more central focus of the labour/wages/trade unions approach in the core.

Aiding and controlling business behaviour

In part, as in all syllabuses, this is considered in the other four areas. The environment, and how it constrains and supports, is treated in section 1, the impact of the law is seen in marketing production and other operational areas. But this syllabus lays more stress than most on responses to business behaviour. This is seen in 2(b), which is devoted to an exploration of the impact that business and society have or attempt to have on each other.

This syllabus certainly does not contradict the view that there is a core to Business Studies, but perhaps it is easy to illustrate from because it sets out to define such a core. The AEB syllabus, in contrast, is a single linear one, with no options, and no attempt to distinguish one part of the syllabus from another. Is there a common core here?

Common core in the AEB syllabus[3]

There are two components of the AEB assessment, but they do not distinguish between areas of the syllabus, neither do they offer study choice to the candidate. The distinction between them lies in the skills being assessed and the techniques of assessment which are used. Once more, we use the same model to look for a common core.

The environment

The syllabus introduction emphasizes the importance of both this and section 5 of our model:

> The syllabus has been drawn up to emphasise the following aspects of the subject:
> (c) the interdependence of the various parts of the business world and of business itself with society and economics, both national and inter-national.[9]

In section 1, which deals with business organizations, there is a guidance note reminding teachers of the need for an historical perspective, but it is in section 5 that full treatment of the environment is given.

Business organization

Many syllabuses start with the environment within which business operates. The AEB does not, choosing to look at the structure and aims of business first. Section one does not fit the model, because it is much wider, stressing time and time again the importance of integrating the strata and themes of the subject. Relating the structure of a business to its objectives takes away the rote learning approach to the different structures and helps to set a problem solving focus.

Business behaviour

It could be argued that this is the focus of the syllabus as a whole, since all aspects are treated dynamically. All elements in our model are present in the syllabus, except production, of which the guidance notes say:

> Production has not been given a separate heading. However, some study of production,

its problems and its inter-relationships with other sections of business and the economy is implicit.[10]

It is in this area of the syllabuses that we would see most difference between our two exemplars. The statement in this syllabus is clear in its intention to sideline production, but is it helpful to teachers? The Cambridge syllabuses take a different view, which includes production, but analysis of this section will demonstrate that it is really costing and ways of making production more efficient through stock control, work study, quality control and value analysis. Analysis of the AEB syllabus and assessment will demonstrate that what they regard as 'implicit' is most, if not all, of these things.

People in business
The AEB treatment of this section is seen largely in Section 4. It differs from that of the Industrial Studies syllabus in that the treatment is micro, concerned with the needs of individual businesses and the practical processes they go through in obtaining and training the workforce they need. Trade unions and collective bargaining are given thorough treatment, and certain aspects of human relations are selected. There is a lack of guidance notes in this section, so it is not entirely clear how extensive the treatment is, or to what extent candidates should be able to refer to the work of theorists.

Aiding and controlling business behaviour
A very strong element of this syllabus. It is reflected in all sections and good guidance is given where a limitation of study is needed. Sections 5 and 6 provide the focus for the approach.

Other syllabuses

The analysis suggests that the model is helpful, and its use with the two examples chosen suggests that there is a common core for the subject. Attitudes to them and their content vary from one course to another. The evidence does not suggest that variations are so extensive as to deny the existence of a common core.

The analysis of other syllabuses using this model would, in my view, lead to similar conclusions. The choice of A level course would seem to depend upon the kind of approach a teacher is seeking or the mode of assessment the syllabus adopts, but there is another issue – how important is a quantitative approach and how should it be reflected in a syllabus?

The numeracy content of a syllabus

Teachers have made decisions between business studies syllabuses on precisely this issue. There are those who have rejected the Cambridge linear syllabus in favour of the AEB one because the former is 'too mathematical' or 'has too much numeracy in it'. How important is it to treat this subject quantitatively?

If we are to use the business context as the basis for developing skills of problem solving, there can be no doubt as to the centrality of the ability to collect, present, interpret, use and evaluate all kinds of evidence, some of which must be numerical. Much of that data also need organization and analysis before they can be used effectively. This requires ability to use a range of techniques and to understand what is happening in the process. The student must also be aware that using data in these ways is always part of the process, rather than a way of finding the answer.

It seems necessary to develop and use these skills. The intention of doing so appears in the aims and the assessment objectives of virtually all syllabuses. The syllabuses do accept that numerate skills and therefore their expression within the content to be studied are part of the essential core. As with other areas of content, we see marked differences of emphasis. The Cambridge linear gives strong emphasis to 'quantitative skills and understanding' but only in the context of business behaviour or of problem solving, and never for its own sake. To emphasize this approach, it guarantees that 50 per cent of the marks in paper 1 will be for qualitative understanding of either the problem being addressed or the technique being used. Whilst the AEB syllabus does not overtly stress the importance of these things, there is a significant numerate element in the syllabus. Part of Section 1 concerns 'the use, preparation and interpretation of business data'; section 2 is entirely concerned with accounting, and this includes investment appraisal.

Coursework in the curriculum

All syllabuses stress the value of coursework in the curriculum. It is seen as an important aid to effective learning, enriching and broadening understanding. The difference between the AEB syllabus and others is in the use of coursework as an assessment component. The AEB is alone in not assessing in this way. This stance may well have a strong appeal, since there are many teachers who see coursework as an unnecessary addition to the things that must be done to run an A level course successfully. The lobby for coursework is a strong one, with both educational and assessment arguments to support it. It is not unlikely that the experience of GCSE will increase the preparedness of both teachers and students to look for an assessed coursework component. It is possible that the new form of A level may require a coursework approach.

Some approaches involve coursework assessment in more than one way and on more than one occasion, but the commoner pattern is a single problem-solving investigation presented in the form of a report and attracting 20–25 per cent of the total mark awarded. In all cases, it is a compulsory component. One important difference is the extent to which teachers are expected to be involved in the assessment procedures. The Cambridge paper 3 is worth 25 per cent of the marks. Teachers may read the projects and offer informal comments about them, but they are not required to be involved in the assessment. This is undertaken by a team of board-appointed external examiners. In the modular course offered by the same board, teachers mark the research assignments and conduct the oral. Their marks are moderated by a board-appointed team. A similar teacher involvement and board moderation is attached to the Industrial Studies approach. In all the others, a strong element of teacher participation is involved.

There is no doubt that coursework not only enriches a course and extends its educational value, it also contributes extensively to examination success. In part, this is because validating what they learn in the classroom motivates students, in part it is a result of the use they can make of the project experience in answering questions. Both these advantages are more likely to accrue where the coursework involves investigation and involvement outside the school environment, ideally within an organization.

All syllabuses assessing through coursework stress that there is no prescription of the kind of organization within which a coursework assignment can be undertaken.

Breadth and depth

'Each part of the syllabus should be studied only in sufficient detail to allow the more complex whole to emerge'. The words are taken from the guidance notes for the Industrial Studies syllabus, but they embody a common perception of how Business Studies should be taught.[10] Students have to know enough to interpret the design of the building and put the bricks into place, but it is the building itself which really matters.

There are certain areas of study to which most syllabuses adopt a common attitude and give some guidance as to breadth and depth. Among these are:

- The environment of business. Not really important for its own sake, and it can well be taught as an integral part of the behavioural areas of business rather than discretely. A broad understanding of the main aspects of that environment is more valuable than a detailed understanding of one element. For example, it is easy to over-teach the macro-economic environment, providing an economist's understanding of it rather than a general management understanding.
- The details of different types of business organization are not normally required. More important are the reasons why a firm may use one form of legal structure rather than another. This is particularly important in company structure, where details of formation procedures, required documents or the provisions of the legislation are not expected, although understanding of principles such as limited liability, continuity and legal personality are.
- Communications is listed as a topic in some syllabuses, whilst in others it is expected to be taught in a range of contents. The theoretical elements of communications are an important part of the Cambridge linear syllabus, but not of the others. None of them require any detailed understanding of the technology.
- Study of the methods and technology of production is required in the Industrial Studies syllabus, but in others treatment is not required and

aspects such as work study, quality control, value analysis and stock control need only be treated descriptively.

- In accounting, in all syllabuses, the approach is not that of book-keeping. Books of account and procedures involved need not be studied. The understanding sought relates to some procedures like costing, budgeting and decision making and to the interpretation of final accounts.
- Wherever there is legislation, no syllabus requires detailed knowledge of the Acts themselves. They do require a knowledge of the objectives of such legislation, something of the way it operates and what the consequences might be.
- Numerate areas of the syllabus are subsumed within most syllabuses, and all those currently on offer stress that quantitative methods are tools to be used. A mathematician's or a statistician's understanding or way of expressing these ideas is not required. Students should be able to select appropriate methods of presentation or techniques of analysis and use them accurately. They should be able to discuss the nature and use of such tools, as well as their strengths and weaknesses in different contexts. The relative importance of this aspect of Business Studies is greatest in the Cambridge linear syllabus. For those teachers who wish to teach it, quantitative methods is an option in the Cambridge modular course and, if selected, greatly increases its importance. Even there, it is contextual and problem-solving understanding which is sought. All syllabuses, however, attach importance to this element.

Other indicators

The syllabus itself contains a number of clues of the kind mentioned above, and these are considerable when there are also notes for guidance available. More recent syllabuses have notes for guidance within them. The Cambridge linear and the Industrial Studies course are both supported by an organization set up for the purpose, and extensive guidance materials can be obtained from them. Addresses are given at the end of this chapter.[11] Other valuable sources of help in this respect are:

- Past papers. These are of greatest help when they are accompanied by solutions. There is growing pressure for mark schemes to be made available, and it is likely that this will happen soon. For the moment, Cambridge solution ideas are provided by the Cambridge Business Studies Project.
- The results of your own students will provide good overall guidance. You can improve on this by pre-request to the examination board for a report on the work of your candidates.
- Examiner's reports. Exam boards produce reports which are helpful to teachers, containing both general observations and question by question analysis.
- Self-help groups. There are now many of these around the country, and how and to what extent particular topics can or should be taught is often the purpose of a meeting.
- INSET. There are many courses, lasting from one day through to one

week, within which questions of breadth and depth are always being considered. Some of these are run by the boards themselves, some as part of local authority provision, some by specialist training groups. If you can identify your own INSET needs, it is likely that one of these organizations will be able to help.

Information Technology in the curriculum

There are three questions here:

1. How far should it be taught in the syllabus?
2. To what extent should it be used by students during the course?
3. What is its role for teaching and learning outcomes?

Should it be taught?

If the answer to this is 'yes', it must surely be a short term one. Many students come to this course having developed IT skills to a high level of competence, and it is to be hoped that none will be without them soon. Most courses assume that the skills will be taught elsewhere and do not include IT as an assessable element. There are two notable exceptions to this general view, which will afford teachers an opportunity to combine Business Studies and IT as assessed components. These two A levels are the London-based BIS course and the Cambridge-based Enfield scheme.

Student use?

Syllabuses, other than the two mentioned above, do not require use, but so many things are easier to understand, better presented and more accurately performed if students do use modern technology. The obvious example of this is coursework, particularly where graphics will enrich the presentation. For larger pieces of work, the editing potential is also a massive advantage. There is no built-in assessment advantage for those who word process their work; the advantages, considerable as they are, are for the student in completing work and modifying it.

Teacher use?

I would find it difficult to run a Business Studies course without considerable use of IT. It is invaluable in preparing work, in modifying it later, in preparing resource material. It revolutionizes the teaching of accounting, and enables me to give students opportunity for supported self-study. It can be used as a support base for case study. I confess disappointment at the quality of most of the teaching software so far produced, but judicious pre-examination and careful thought about objectives can be of help. Two problems frequently arise; the first concerns resources. Access to workstations when they are needed is not always easy and when they are available there are often too few and this causes work management problems. The second problem is time.

Many of these approaches take too much time in the classroom and success therefore depends on access to facilities for students outside contact time.

Information Technology should really be the penmanship of our time, and we should make as much use of it as we can. Problems will arise when students have different skill levels and motivations in using the equipment.

Future developments

The nature of A level and the features of an A level syllabus are both matters of major debate. A new form will emerge in a few years, and there is little point in playing guessing games about it. The ability of A level courses to meet the needs of a much wider range of students whilst maintaining the standards at the top is one of the major debates, but issues such as modular courses, and the inclusion of coursework may also prove to be significant.

Notes

1   UCLES Business Studies A Level Syllabus 1971 et seq.
2   AEB A Level Syllabus 1976 et seq.
3   AEB A Level Business Studies Syllabus 1989.
4   UCLES Business Studies Syllabus 9370 1991.
5   ODLE Industrial Studies Syllabus 1990.
6   Business and Information Studies Coursebook 1990.
7   UCLES Business Studies Syllabus 9514. 1991.
8   SEAC: National Subject Specific Criteria: Business Studies 1984.
9   AEB Syllabus Introduction.
10   AEB Syllabus Teacher Guidance Notes.

9 New Developments in Business Studies at A/S Level

David Dyer

Introduction

Two potential courses of study are available at Advanced level in Business Studies. One of them is discussed in Chapter 8, and most exam boards now have or are developing at least one course of that type. The second course is the Advanced Supplementary (A/S), in which the choice is not yet as wide.

It is important to see A/S courses in this light, and to accept that they are of A level standard. They are designed to be studied over two years in half the contact time devoted to A level. The only feature which should distinguish them from A level is that they contain about half the content of A level courses. All the A level courses have an A/S level associated with them, except the Oxford and Cambridge 'Shared Business Experience' course and the Cambridge Enfield one. In some cases, the A/S is a specially written course, eg Cambridge linear and AEB. In others, it is a designated sub-set of the A level syllabus. Some have coursework; others do not.

Courses available

The AEB course[1]

The main characteristics are as follows:

- The underlying theme is the interaction of business with its environment. The way business operates is not part of the course, beyond those elements which are necessary to achieve the stated objective.
- It is designed to emphasize the same three features that are associated with the A level syllabus:
  (1) the diversity of business activity; (2) the fact of continuing change; (3) interdependence of business and the society of which it is a part.
- Like most A/S syllabuses, it is set out in the more comprehensive modern form, with stated assessment objectives and a clear indication of their relative importance within each component. Teachers may find these useful when considering the full A level as well.
- The pattern of assessment is almost the same as the A level. There are two components of equal weight. Within the first, there are structured questions and no choice. There are no short answer questions of the type found in Section A of the A level papers. Paper 2 is the same, with section A as a

case study and section B a choice from a number of free response questions.
- There is no coursework.
- At first sight, the content of the course seems very similar to the A level, but teachers must bear in mind the environmental objectives of the course and teach in the light of those. The good guidance notes assist with this.
- The need for integrated study is stressed, and section six of the syllabus is designed to promote this.
- Specimen papers and marking guidelines are available from the Board.[1] Again, teachers may find these guidelines helpful in thinking about the way in which full A level papers might be marked and the breadth and depth of teaching. (See the discussion in Chapter 8).

The Cambridge linear course[2]

The main characteristics are:
- The approach reflects the A level syllabus as a whole, containing the central elements of that syllabus. It contains both theory and application.
- It retains the decision-making theme which characterizes the A level approach.
- As the aims and assessment objectives emphasize, it is a skills-based approach.
- There are two written components of the examination. Paper 1 retains, in Part A, the strong numerate element integrated within an approach which is problem solving and requires qualitative understanding of the techniques employed. Part (B) of this component is free response questions testing the whole syllabus. The second component is a case study carrying 40 per cent of the total marks.
- There is no coursework.
- The content is divided into three themes:
  (1) Decision making. It follows the decision-making model, which can be found in the A level syllabus,[3] but is not printed with this one. Both syllabuses are printed in the same booklet.
  (2) Marketing and production.
  (3) Finance and accounting.
- There are excellent notes for guidance which are printed alongside the topics and give clear indications of coverage and relationships.
- Specimen papers and marking guidelines are available.

Cambridge modular course[2]

The main characteristics are as follows:
- The course was structured from the beginning so that the A level course contained within it the components of the A/S one. The first year of study for the A level is also the A/S course, but it is expected that candidates for the A/S will take two years to complete the course. It can be presented in one year, but if that is the first year of post-16 it is not normally successful.

- Since the course is modular, assessment is during the course at the end of each completed module.
- The first module, called the double module, because teaching time and assessment weighting for it are both doubled, is a 'core' approach to Business Studies containing all the elements delineated as 'core' in Chapter 8. It is exactly the same content and approach as the A level. It is worth two thirds of the marks awarded for the A/S. It is expected that candidates will be examined on this work in November of year 2.[4] They can resit in March of year 2.
- The second module is a research assignment, which is an extensive report based on attachment to a local organization, and exactly similar in nature to the Cambridge linear A level project, though the assessment is different. This is worth one third of the marks. It is expected that it will be presented in June of year 2.[5]
- The double module is assessed by appointed external examiners. The research assignment is assessed by the teacher and is externally moderated. The assessment is 70 per cent on the report itself and 25 per cent for an oral on the report. It is stressed that the oral is a further opportunity to assess the report in a different way, and is not intended to test oral or presentation skills.
- There are extensive notes for guidance in the syllabus.[2]
- The originators of the course, the board and the Cambridge Business Studies Project all offer INSET for this course.[6]
- It is possible for A/S candidates who are performing well to transfer to the A course and vice versa for those overstretched at A level.[7]
- One of the features of the modular course is that results can be banked and modules can be taken again over a period of five years.
- The administration is complex and teachers must familiarize themselves with the regulations well before setting out on the course.[8]

Oxford course[8]

The main characteristics are:

- It is an Industrial Studies course strongly retaining the approach of its companion A level. Like all the others, it is presented in the modern style and as such is much more teacher friendly than the A level syllabus.
- The content is a sub-set of the A level course.
- It is stressed in several places that it is an integrated course, the whole being the objective of teaching the parts.
- It is a skills-based approach, with emphasis in the aims on practical skills, personal confidence, decision making and concepts.
- The focus is manufacturing, and the production elements of Business Studies are more central to this than to other syllabuses.
- The whole syllabus is examined through one component, lasting 3 hours and worth 80 per cent of the total mark awarded. Part A of this is two

compulsory case studies. Part B is four free response questions, from which two must be chosen.

- The second component is coursework, worth 20 per cent of the total marks awarded, and is either a single report on an investigation or a comparison of an aspect of theory with the reality within a given organization.[9]
- Paper 1 is externally assessed, but the Project is teacher-assessed and board-moderated.
- The focus of the content is the 'organization', and all elements of the course are related to that with a diagram to demonstrate how. Section A of the study is the environment of the organization and Section B, aspects of its operations. It is similar to the A level core.
- There are extensive notes for guidance provided by the support group.

London Business and Information Studies course[10]

The GCSE in Business and Information Studies is by the far the biggest of the courses available at that level. Some readers may be familiar with it as the Hampshire Project. The A level and A/S courses developed from this are 'pilot courses', which means that entry to them is controlled for the first few years, whilst progress and development are monitored.

The main characteristics are:

- The stress, in the rationale and objectives, on experiential approaches to learning.
- The importance placed on the local community as a major resource for learning.
- Like many other courses, the focus on problem solving and decision making.
- Common experience in both business and technological education treated as a unified whole.
- The continuous nature of the assessment process, its integration within the approach to learning and the use of criterion-referencing.
- A national and regional network of support for teachers together with appropriate INSET.
- The content is expressed as a central core – 'the Business Plan' – around which a range of option modules are available. These follow the pattern of the A level and provide a wide but rigorous choice, reflecting all the main areas of business activity. There is also a range of wider options from which one must be selected and which, *inter alia*, can give opportunity to study 'Languages in Business' or 'Business and Media Design'.
- Assessment is on coursework. Each module is assessed both through a portfolio of work related to it and through assessment of groupwork.
- The assessment structure involves the student and the teacher very much more completely in the assessment process than is true for other courses. Many teachers will welcome this direct participation. They will certainly welcome the training and support mechanisms which make it possible.
- The course assumes a knowledge of word processing and associated skills.
- There is a resource requirement. Course developers recommend a ratio of

three students per workstation and also recommend software packages.

- The aims and assessment objectives associated with each module are well defined as are the levels of response expected. The content of the course is not specified in any greater detail. This is inevitable and to some extent desirable in a skills-based, flexible course, but teachers new to the subject area may not feel entirely confident of the nature and extent of the learning they must enable.

The value of A/S courses

Examination groups were relatively slow to develop supplementary level courses in Business Education. In part this was probably because most boards had only small entries for the full A level, and remained to be convinced of the market for the A/S. Although there are now a range of different A/S courses available, providing a real choice for everyone, candidate numbers are universally low, a fact not confined to Business Studies alone.

Some reasons for this are:

- Many teachers of Business Studies are new to the subject and need to gain confidence and experience before they tackle yet another new course.
- Business Studies is not easy to adapt to the A/S approach. It is difficult to know what to leave out and to what depth the ideas which are included should be pursued. There is a danger that far too much will be crammed into a course in order to be certain.
- Courses are always easier to pursue when they have passed the development stage: past papers become available, resources are written, experienced advice can be sought, INSET begins to appear.
- There is a substantial shortage of teachers of Business Studies.
- A level has grown at a remarkable rate in the past few years. All the teachers and resources a school or college possesses are committed to its delivery.

In this situation, where the opportunity cost of committing resources to an A/S course is high, teachers have to be convinced that such a course will be in demand and will enrich the provision which the school or college makes. Teachers and those who advise on further education opportunities also have to be certain that A/S courses will be fully acceptable.

The strongest argument for A/S Business Studies lies in the push for a senior school curriculum which has a broader base. The contribution which the subject can make to general as well as specialist education is well argued elsewhere in this volume and does not need reinforcement. But the pattern of full A levels which students either need or wish to follow will have room for Business Studies in only a sub-set of the year group. The others can only avail themselves of the opportunities of this subject area if it can be provided in a smaller course or in a general studies programme. These arguments are, of course, the ones upon which the development of A/S courses in general is founded, but they apply with particular force to subjects like Business Studies, which tend to combine the features of 'arts' and 'science' courses. There are, however, some subject specific justifications:

- The subject is now a major one in further education institutions which increasingly attracts the attention and interest of young people. It is no longer the poor relation of A level provision.
- It integrates qualitative and quantitative understanding, operating within a problem-solving and decision-making approach. This can be applied to other studies; mature skills may be developed in other contexts and greatly assist the transfer of skills matured in specific disciplines into a wider use.
- It has shown itself to be particularly adaptable to the student-centred, coursework and modular approaches.
- It greatly increases the sense of a school or college as part of the community and is rich in opportunities to work within the community as an integral part of the course of study.

Choosing A/S level courses

It is no part of this chapter to undertake a consumer survey and emerge with a *Which?* best buy, but we can pose the main questions which might assist choice. There are three models on offer, and some of the courses combine features of more than one of them:

(1) The traditional end-of-course examination as the sole vehicle of assessment. This applies to both the AEB course and the Cambridge linear A/S.
(2) The course which is assessed partly or wholly through coursework. Opportunities here range from the 20 per cent of the Oxford course to the 100 per cent of BIS.
(3) Modular courses which are sub-sets of the A level course and may be tempting as a stepping stone to A level or a fall back position for those who find the going tough. It must be stressed, however, that these are not the justification for courses at this level. They are specifically designed for those whose objective is A/S rather than for those who might fall back to it. On the other hand, there may be an attraction in this model because it permits extension forward into a full A level for those who have gained an added interest or demonstrated a capability.

Why are students taking the course? Students who are following a course because they are of full A level potential and wish to develop a broader base will be developing A level skills in other subjects and may be likely to reach the required standard. They may well complete the course in a year, but are more likely to do so successfully in their second A level year or in later education. For them, the linear examination may well be the most appropriate. Students who are taking the course because they need to tackle the lower content and to mature skills steadily within that smaller content may well need to take the full two years over the course, and benefit from waiting until the end before they are assessed. Again, this points to a linear traditional approach. The modular course might be best for those who respond to continuous assessment and work best towards short regular targets. The modular approach also suits those who work well on their own and will use non-contact time well.

What other objectives do they have? If one of the objectives is A level Business Studies, then one of the courses which permits movement through A/S to A level may be the right choice. This will also be the case where the objective is as yet unknown and the student needs to settle into and respond to the subject before the best objective becomes clear. On the other hand, too heavy a burden of coursework is often more than students can handle, particularly if they already have such commitments in more than one subject. These factors may militate against both modular courses and ones which have projects.

What are students' strengths and weaknesses? These may not be revealed until a course is chosen, but different courses present features like extended projects which benefit those who can work on their own, have learnt how to research and can write a good report. Others provide opportunity for case study work. Those who have demonstrated that they work best under controlled examination conditions will benefit from a traditional approach.

One factor often considered by teachers is the relative importance of quantitative skills within a syllabus. Quite rightly, there is no syllabus within which the ability to use and understand number can be entirely avoided, but the only one which makes a significant feature of such skills is the Cambridge linear.[11]

How much time will you have? Many A/S courses are undertaken with insufficient time or with students in groups with others taking the full A level. In these circumstances a course which maximises the opportunities for supported self-study is needed.

What resources are available? Not likely to be an important consideration for A/S level, since none of the courses available, except BIS, has any specific resource implications. But the Cambridge courses, the Oxford course and BIS have support projects through which specially written resources are made available to teachers and by which INSET courses are often provided.

The role of the teacher. What role do you as a teacher feel able and willing to play? Some courses heavily involve the teacher in the assessment of the course, and for the Cambridge modular and BIS there is considerable administration. The amount of administration or the need to find project placements should never really be a consideration, set against the quality and appropriateness of a course, but they may well be positive or negative factors if other things are equal. The value to teacher and student of a teacher's involvement in assessment is enormous, and courses which offer a high degree of teacher participation may well be popular for that reason alone.

Teacher experience. Confidence comes from experience. Some courses will not be popular with teachers because they are not confident of delivering them effectively. Teachers with no specific training in the subject area and with no experience of teaching it are often asked to do so. It is one of the penalties associated with developing subject areas. For teachers in this position, modular courses may pose a problem. Modules are assessed after a very short time, and they offer no leeway for the teacher to realize that things are not quite right and re-teach a topic or an area. One of the most difficult things for a teacher new to the subject to do is to identify ways in which the course may be integrated, topics taught together which it takes longer to teach apart, subjects which may reasonably be left out, or associations of topics which promote understanding. All of these matters may be reasons for avoiding modular approaches. They may also be reasons for avoiding courses with projects. Many teachers become concerned about the role they have when students are undertaking assignment work, and also worry about the appropriateness of titles and approaches which students might adopt. It is tempting to leave such concerns to others, if the opportunity arises. An inexperienced teacher will value most the advice and support of others, so this may suggest a course for which there is an identified source of advice and guidance or one which is being offered by another school in the locality. There may be opportunities for cooperative working or shared resources. There will certainly be a source of help.

Conclusion

A/S courses are developing and establishing their credentials. There is no one best course, but, fortunately, modern syllabuses are quite helpful and informative documents and all teachers can find the course they most want to teach in a particular environment. It would be wrong to treat an A/S course as a soft option or as a course for the 'less able'. Most students will substantially underachieve if they are asked to complete an A/S course as the first year of study after GCSE. The intellectual level of A/S is as high as A level, and if there are some courses and some results obtained through them which do not give that impression, it is only a matter of time before teachers realize this.

Notes

1 Syllabus from AEB, Stag House, Guildford GU2 5XL.
2 Syllabus available from UCLES, 1 Hills Road, Cambridge CB1 2EU.
3 Cambridge syllabus booklet–Syllabus No 9370.
4 Candidates for the full A level will normally sit in March of year 1. Candidates attempting A/S in a single year would also have to sit the double module in March of year 1.
5 Candidates taking the A level can submit in either June of year 1 or October of year 2.
6 The Cambridge Business Studies Project–Culm House, 22 Nene Crescent, Oakham LE15 6SG. The Peterborough Modular Group, P E D C, Cottesmore Place, Peterborough.
7 It is also possible for candidates to be awarded an A/S certificate on the way to A level but both cannot be awarded in the same year.
8 Syllabus from OUDLE, Oxford.
9 There is a subject support group at the Teacher Training Department of Warwick University. Extensive guidance, particularly on the project, and in-service training are provided.
10 Syllabus available from ULSEB, Stewart House, Russell Square, London.
11 A new course is being developed by JMB, which also has a high numerate content.

10 Business Education and the National Curriculum

Steven Blowers

Requirements of the Education Reform Act (ERA) 1988

The ERA established a National Curriculum for 5 to 16 year olds, consisting of three core and seven foundation subjects. Neither Business Studies nor Economics was identified as one of these subjects, but this does not imply that business education will be absent from the curriculum once the full effects of the ERA are upon us.

Technology is one of the foundation subjects, divided into two profile components; design and technology capability and information technology capability (IT) (DES, 1990a). Non-statutory guidance published to assist and support teachers, comments that 'design and technology is not an amalgam of existing subjects, but teachers of art and design, business education, craft design and technology (CDT), home economics, information technology/computer studies have vital contributions to make'. Referring more specifically to business education, 'design and technology includes aspects of economic and industrial understanding, such as researching, planning, budgeting, marketing and managing. The programmes of study [for design and technology] allow for work outside school and, at Key Stage 4, for work experience' (NCC, 1990a).

The ERA refers to a requirement for a 'balanced and broadly based curriculum', which includes preparation for 'the opportunities, responsibilities and experiences of adult life'. This has provided the rationale for the inclusion of a number of cross-curricular themes and skills as an integral part of the whole curriculum, identified by the National Curriculum Council (NCC, 1990b). Education for economic and industrial understanding is one of these themes; 'an essential part of every pupil's curriculum. It helps pupils understand the world in which they live and prepares them for life and work in a rapidly changing, economically competitive world. It is needed in all key stages' (NCC, 1990c).

The desire for a broad, balanced and relevant curriculum has led to the view that at Key Stage 4, pupils need to be able to have a degree of choice between courses. Not all foundation subjects may be required to be followed by all pupils, and it is likely to be possible to combine subjects in a single GCSE course (DES 1990b). Time will therefore be available for additional non-core and foundation subjects to be offered at Key Stage 4, and many pupils will continue to follow GCSE courses in Business Studies or Economics.

Clearly, there is scope and potential for the development of business education in the whole curriculum 5–16 following the ERA. Business education teachers will be working in teams with colleagues from many other subject backgrounds to team teach, develop appropriate learning materials and map where elements of the curriculum (eg, programmes of study, themes and skills) are being delivered and developed across the whole curriculum, to ensure a genuinely broad and balanced experience for all pupils. Overall, there will be a growing presence for business education in the curriculum in the years ahead.

The challenge will be for schools to adopt a broader view of business education. In the past, in the 5–16 curriculum, business education has often been seen as confined to options at GCSE (eg, Accounting, Business Studies, Commerce, Economics, Keyboarding, Office Practice). All pupils between the ages of 5 and 16 are entitled to a business education experience (through National Curriculum subjects and cross-curricular themes), and may choose to study a business education subject which conforms to GCSE National Criteria (ie, Business Studies or Economics) in greater depth at Key Stage 4. The Training Agency has published a business education handbook for schools, which seeks to encourage good practice, and a whole-school policy on business education. 'The ideal approach for any whole school policy . . . is to merge the two perspectives of economics and business [studies] so that they feed off each other and enrich the curriculum for all' (Training Agency, 1990).

Developing business education in the school . . . depend[s] heavily for [its] success on several key factors, including:

• staff awareness of potential business and economic perspectives in their subjects
• staff commitment to the idea of developing such perspectives
• flexible, pupil-centred approaches to the teaching–learning process
• staff capacity to work in teams when dealing with cross-curricular [themes]
• the existence of a timetable mechanism for ensuring coherence, continuity and progression in business education throughout the school.

These key factors need to be underpinned by effective staff development, sensitive timetabling, and continuing leadership from senior management (ibid.)

Business education in the curriculum 5–16

Contribution to Design and Technology

Pupils should be taught a programme of study for Design and Technology, specified for each of the key stages. Business education teachers will have no difficulty in recognizing elements of these programmes, in particular those which relate to 'developing and communicating ideas' and 'satisfying needs and addressing opportunities' (DES 1990a).

In each key stage pupils should design and make:

- artefacts (objects made by people);
- systems (sets of objects or activities which together perform a task);
- environments (surroundings made, or developed, by people);

in response to needs and opportunities identified by them.

Contexts (situations in which design and technological activity takes place) should include the home, school, recreation, community, business and industry, beginning with those which are most familiar to pupils, and progressing to contexts which are less familiar.

These activities should also reflect (a pupil's) growing understanding of the needs and beliefs of other people and cultures, now and in the past.

As pupils progress, they should be given more opportunities to identify their own tasks for activity, and should use their knowledge and skills to make products which are more complex, or satisfy more demanding needs (DES, 1990a).

Design and Technology is sub-divided into four attainment targets (ATs) for assessment purposes

- AT1   identifying needs and opportunities
- AT2   generating a design
- AT3   planning and making
- AT4   evaluating

each with a number of statements of attainment at different levels, illustrated in Figure 10.1.

Pupils should be able to:

- use the results of investigations to identify needs
- consider both the user and the producer when defining the need for technological activity
- seek out, appraise, organize and use information from different sources
- adopt procedures which pay regard to cost
- review the decision-making process used in producing their final artefact, system or environment
- understand the social and economic implications of some artefacts, systems or environments
- evaluate their product in relation to the original needs, taking into account users' views, cost-effectiveness and scale of production
- illustrate the economic, moral, social and environmental consequences of design and technological innovations including some from the past and other cultures.

Figure 10.1 *Examples of statements of attainment for Design and Technology capability*
Source: DES, 1990a

The introduction of Technology as a foundation subject will ensure that elements of business education are related to the design and making (production) of artefacts, systems and environments for all pupils between the ages of 5 and 16. This represents a welcome extension of business education experiences to a wider age group of pupils than we have seen before in primary and secondary schools.

Contribution to cross-curricular themes and skills

The NCC has identified five 'pre-eminent' themes which, 'it is reasonable to assume . . . are essential parts of the whole curriculum' for all pupils 5–16 (NCC, 1990b):

- economic and industrial understanding
- careers education and guidance
- health education
- education for citizenship
- environmental education.

The Training Agency (1990) comments, 'some of these themes may be delivered in whole, or in part, through business education'. It takes a broader view of education for economic and industrial understanding, using the phrase, 'business and economic understanding', for which it proposes a definition:

> The term Business and Economic Understanding can be applied to those curriculum activities which are aimed at raising pupils' understanding of core business and economic issues, developing their capacity to make informed judgements on such issues and giving them the confidence to take appropriate action. The term can also apply to activities aimed at improving pupils' business skills. The curriculum activities concerned may be cross-curricular, modular or subject based. Their overall effect is to provide pupils with a strong sense of the Business and Economic perspectives that underlie all their school subjects as well as much of what goes on outside school in the community at large (ibid.).

The NCC comments that education for economic and industrial understanding should enable pupils to 'have direct experience of industry and the world of work and take part in small-scale business and community enterprise projects' (NCC, 1990b). This is extended in the Training Agency's handbook, in chapters on 'enterprise education' and 'managing links with employer organisations'. 'Enterprise education [seeks] to develop enterprising skills amongst pupils, using the framework of a business operation to develop widely-applicable skills and attitudes, such as conducting an enquiry, working collaboratively, and showing initiative'. One of the objectives a school might set for planning links with local businesses and employers might be 'to enrich the curriculum as a whole by bringing the external world of work into the school, in the form of adults other than teachers, contextual materials, problems to be solved etc. (Training Agency, 1990). Business educationalists may also consider some aspects of consumer education to be appropriate in this context.

The NCC has also identified a number of core skills which it considers essential to develop 'across the whole curriculum (5–16) in a measured and planned way' (NCC, 1990b):

- communication skills (oracy and literacy)
- numeracy
- problem solving and study skills
- personal and social skills
- IT

Business education teachers will be able to contribute to the development of all of these skills. In particular, many will be able to contribute to the development of a pupil's Information Technology capability (one of the two profile components within the foundation subject of Technology). IT should not be viewed as a content element within a business education course, but as a tool which should be used (for example in decision making and problem solving) to enhance learning.

Progression in the development of skills is important; 'the programmes of study [for IT] are the minimum entitlement for all pupils' (NCC, 1990d) and increasingly it will be possible to build on pupils' experience in each key stage. Pupils will have acquired the ability to use IT in a range of curriculum contexts in Key Stage 3; it will, therefore, be possible to build on this at age 14 and to use more sophisticated IT applications in GCSE Business Studies and Economics courses. For those students post-16 who do not have experience of a business education GCSE course, the entitlement to a curriculum with an element of economic and industrial understanding and IT during each key stage will better prepare them for beginning business education courses at age 16.

Business education teachers will have much to contribute to the development and teaching of cross-curricular themes and skills:

> A business education department which has well-trained staff, ample materials for business and economic applications, and a solid base of office technology, is in a strong position to make a substantial contribution to the teaching of business and economic understanding and business related IT to all pupils. There is certainly no current evidence to suggest that high quality cross-curricular work can be achieved in the absence of specialist expertise and resources (Training Agency, 1990).

Key Stage 4

There are likely to be changes in GCSE provision at Key Stage 4 over the next few years, influenced primarily by developments in the National Curriculum, although it is likely that GCSEs in Business Studies and Economics will continue to be available in a similar form to those currently available. The opportunity to combine subjects at GCSE will be significant for business education, and there are likely to be some interesting developments. There are already a number of GCSE Business Studies syllabuses which offer a range of optional components, for example the SEG 'core plus options' syllabus offers an option in a modern foreign language, LEAG syllabus B offers an option in Economics, and a number of syllabuses (the previous two included) offer options in IT. GCSE syllabuses in the future are likely to combine Business Studies and Economics with National Curriculum subjects, provided that these courses 'are rigorous and conform with the [National Curriculum subject's] attainment targets and programmes of study' (DES, 1990b). It will be important to view such courses in an integrated way, rather than as combinations of two unrelated subjects, and teaching should reflect this.

Perhaps two of the most significant developments will be GCSE courses in Business Studies with a modern foreign language and Business Studies with

Information Systems. Linking Business Studies with a modern foreign language has an obvious relevance. Britain lags behind other European countries in language skills, and there is a need to look ahead to the challenge of the Single European Market and the opportunity that people will have to live and work in any part of the European Community. It would be appropriate to offer pupils the opportunity to acquire their information systems capability within an extended business education context, as there are many business education elements within the attainment targets and programme of study for design and technology at Key Stage 4. It is possible to consider other combinations, for example, Economics with Geography, and there has in the past been a GCE 'O' Level course in Business Studies with an option in Economic and Social History.

The increasing number of pupils taking GCSE courses in business education subjects over the last five years would seem to suggest that a range of new GCSE courses which combine an element of business education with a National Curriculum subject would be popular with pupils. Other opportunities also exist, for example, programmes are available which aim to add a pre-vocational or vocational element to the 14-16 curriculum (see Chapter 11). Business education teachers will, in many instances, need to acquire new skills, but this has always been the case, and these developments should be seen as an opportunity to extend and enrich the business education experience offered to pupils in the curriculum at Key Stage 4.

Team teaching approaches

Although the ERA will bring about a widening of the business education experience in the curriculum to include all pupils between the ages of 5 and 16, business education specialists are likely to be involved primarily in Key Stages 3 and 4, in Design and Technology, education for economic and industrial understanding and option subjects at GCSE.

Business education teachers need to work with colleagues from Art and Design, CDT and Home Economics to plan and deliver Design and Technology in Key Stages 3 and 4. Traditionally, business education has not been taught as a subject in Years 7, 8 and 9, and there may not be sufficient specialists to be involved in the teaching of Design and Technology in all of these year groups. The involvement of business education teachers in planning curriculum materials is essential, however, if the business perspective required for Design and Technology activities is to be realistic and meaningful. This is not a curriculum area in which four subjects and IT are taught separately from each other. Attempts to develop approaches to the delivery of Design and Technology which aim to teach about business divorced from a design-and-make context or which encourage the acquisition of craft or other skills in isolation, should be strongly resisted. Integration can be achieved by relating class activity to a theme – products and packaging for example – and pupils should be given the opportunity to research and to identify their own tasks for designing and making, including visits and work outside school. This does not mean, however, that a pupil's learning should be so unstructured that the experience lacks coherence or rigour.

Working with colleagues from a range of subject backgrounds, business education teachers will need to determine which elements within education for economic and industrial understanding (and other appropriate cross-curricular themes) are currently being offered in a school's curriculum, and identify which elements are missing and need, therefore, to be included. This will allow a curriculum map to be produced, in line with the whole-school policy for business education, which identifies where in the curriculum all the elements within education for economic and industrial understanding are being delivered to all pupils in each key stage. An important role for the business education specialist will be to assist colleagues in interpreting the elements within education for economic and industrial understanding, to suggest ways in which they might successfully be delivered in the classroom, and to assist in the development of curriculum materials. This process will also apply to the development of an IT (and other skills) policy within a school; it will no longer be acceptable to offer some pupils in Year 10 an experience of IT within a GCSE Business Studies course and no, or very little, IT experience to the remainder.

The teams planning (and developing) materials for both Design and Technology and cross-curricular themes and skills need to take into account continuity and progression. Within each key stage, pupils must be given the opportunity to develop their skills, knowledge and abilities in a planned way, allowing them to move on when they are able and return to areas of difficulty if necessary. Business educationalists may well lead some or all of these teams, but they have no special claim over others to do so; coordinators for Design and Technology, IT and education for economic and industrial understanding should be appointed on the basis of an individual's interest, skills and time commitments elsewhere in the curriculum.

Planning for the delivery of National Curriculum subjects, cross-curricular themes and skills and option subjects, should take place within the context of the whole curriculum, through a process of curriculum mapping (a curriculum audit) and whole-curriculum development plans (NCC, 1990b). A whole-school policy for business education, referring to Design and Technology, education for economic and industrial understanding (enterprise education, links with employer organizations and other appropriate cross-curricular themes), the development of business-related IT and other skills, and business education GCSE courses (Business Studies and Economics), should be seen in the context of the whole curriculum of which it is a part.

References

DEA (1990a) *Technology in the National Curriculum*. HMSO, London.

DES (1990b) *National Curriculum. For 14 to 16 year olds.* Speech by the Secretary of State for Education and Science, 25 January. DES, London.

NCC (1990a) *Non-statutory Guidance. Design & Technology Capability*. National Curriculum Council, York.

NCC (1990b) *Curriculum Guidance 3. The Whole Curriculum*. National Curriculum Council, York.
NCC (1990c) *Curriculum Guidance 4. Education for Economic and Industrial Understanding*. National Curriculum Council, York.
NCC (1990d) *Non-statutory Guidance, Information Technology Capability*. National Curriculum Council, York.
Training Agency (1990) *Business Education. A Handbook for Schools*. Training Agency TVEI Teacher Support Unit, Sheffield.

11 GCSE Business Studies

Ian Chambers

The development of GCSE Business Studies

> The uncertain position of industry stands out from the history of education in Britain. Elite educational institutions, from the Victorian era on . . . reflected and propagated an anti-industrial bias. The genteel pattern of later Victorian public schools was fixed (one level lower) on the new state grammar schools from their establishment by the Education Act of 1902. Similarly, the ancient universities served as a powerful model for state-provided higher education in the twentieth century. The University of Oxford, one science don complained, in 1903, 'has always ostentatiously held herself aloof from manufacturing and commerce' (Wiener, 1981).

This 'anti-industrial bias' in British education, as recognized by Wiener, has had an important influence over the place of business education in British schools, giving practical and vocational subjects such as Business Studies a low status in the twentieth century school curriculum. Only in the last five years has the position of Business Studies strengthened in such a way that it has been able to gain a place within Technology, a foundation subject of the National Curriculum of England and Wales.

Goodson has traced the development of high-status and low-status subjects in the school curriculum (Goodson, 1987). High-status knowledge is knowledge that is not immediately useful, but will become professionally vocational at a later stage, eg, the classics, the pure sciences, the arts, history. This knowledge, divided into discrete units in the form of school subjects, has formed the academic tradition which dominated and still dominates the school curriculum. The examination system has reinforced this process from School Certificate (1917) through GCE O and A levels (1951) and CSE Mode 1 syllabuses (1965) to GCSE National Criteria (1985) and National Curriculum Statutory Orders (1989 onwards).

Low-status knowledge is utilitarian knowledge, knowledge useful for the sort of occupations in which most people work, and yet technical and commercial education has never been given the same importance in the school curriculum. High-status subjects have built themselves a vested position in schools, through departments, resources, more able pupils, promotion and incentive posts, headships; through curriculum discrimination. Attempts by low-status subjects to achieve high-status through the examination system were largely unsuccessful until recently. The inclusion of Technology as a National Curriculum foundation subject is the first indication of a change in attitude towards such subjects as Craft, Design and Technology, Business Education and Home Economics. Such a change, however, has come more from government pressure than from school pressure.

This analysis helps to explain two important features in the development of GCSE Business Studies. First, the weak position held by such discrete subjects as Accounts, Commerce, Typewriting and Office Practice in the school curriculum of the 1960s and 1970s, meant that such subjects were only available in 4th and 5th year options and thought appropriate for low-achieving boys (in the case of Commerce and Accounts) and low-achieving girls (in the case of Typewriting and Office Practice). Secondly, curriculum developers within business education wanted to move their subject on to a broader and more academic basis to ensure a stronger place in the curriculum.

This process began in schools with the introduction of an A level in Business Studies which was first examined by the Cambridge Local Examinations Syndicate in 1969. An O level followed in 1978, and schools teaching these syllabuses received curriculum support from the Cambridge Business Studies Project. The focus of development was within the academic/examination curriculum. This was a deliberate aim of the Project, as it did not see such courses as in any way vocational, although the integrated nature of the syllabuses did reflect developments in business education in further education (eg, BEC/BTEC national courses). Similar curriculum support was not provided for a second A level Business Studies course developed by the Associated Examining Board. University acceptance was also seen as important by the Cambridge Project.

Until the mid 1980s, broad based Business Studies found it difficult to maintain a position in the school curriculum. Entries were small and the subject relied on a group of enthusiasts to sustain the development work that had gone on in the 1970s. Few teachers were qualified in the discipline of management science that the syllabuses drew upon and only one post-graduate training course specifically prepared student teachers for broad based Business Studies. The experience of the author was typical; when I left a large Sixth Form College in 1983 to move into teacher training, A level Business Studies disappeared from the option choices after one year as no other teacher felt willing or able to take over the course.

The climate for Business Studies has become much more favourable since the early 1980s. HMI and the DES began to talk in terms of a broad and balanced curriculum, with increased emphasis upon the relevance of what is learnt to the present and future lives of pupils. Business Studies is seen in a more favourable light, as it is easier than, for example, in Economics, for teachers to make 'abstract ideas more concrete and relevant' (Taylor, 1988). Two developments in particular have served to enhance the position of Business Studies in the curriculum – GCSE National Criteria and the Technical and Vocational Education Initiative (TVEI).

In 1985, Business Studies was accepted by the Schools Examinations Council (SEC) as one of the twenty subjects to have National Criteria for the new GCSE examination. This led all examination groups to develop new syllabuses for GCSE Business syllabuses to be presented alongside GCSE Commerce, Accounts and Office Practice syllabuses. Since the first examination of GCSE in 1988, the Business Studies entry has grown steadily, to a large extent at the expense of Accounts and Commerce. Figures below show the continuing growth in contrast to GCSE Economics:

| | Number taking examination | |
	1989	1990
Business Studies GCSE	28957	59177
Economics GCSE	29833	28168

(Source: The Times, 23 August 1990.)

It is now unlikely that for the new set of GCSE syllabuses for the National Curriculum, due in 1995, the Schools Examinations and Assessment Council (SEAC) will allow any syllabuses in this area other than Business Studies and Economics.

The second important development has been TVEI, now being extended to most pupils aged 14–19. The focus of the TVEI pilot projects was to enhance the provision of technical and vocational subjects, and nearly all projects included the enhancement of business education. Indeed, a number of GCSE Business Studies syllabuses owe either their existence or growth to TVEI-enhanced curriculum funding and support in schools and authorities. The Northern Examination Association's Business Studies Syllabus B – a modular syllabus – and Tameside's Mode 3 Business Studies GCSE, certificated by the Midland Examining Group – also modular in nature – were both developed by TVEI pilot teachers working in consortia. The growth of the most successful (in terms of entry) GCSE Business Studies course, that is the Hampshire Business and Information Studies (BIS) Double Option GCSE (now certificated by the London and East Anglia Examining Group – LEAG) owes much to the increased funding that TVEI gave to schools to improve their Information Technology, and the appointment of many advisory teachers in local authorities under TVEI funding, who could support BIS teachers and run coursework moderation.

The emphasis that TVEI placed on process and skill-based approaches to learning fitted well with the nature of business education. The subject lends itself well to the use of simulations, games, role play activities, enterprise activities, visits to industry and work experience. The skills involved in the use of Information Technology have been incorporated into Business Studies curriculum development; the BIS course is the most obvious example, but other syllabuses have also sought to integrate the use of IT into the learning process.

It might also be thought that the growth in business and management courses in higher education has been important in fostering school based developments. However, A level and GCSE Business Studies both developed out of school influences rather than university influence. This contrasts with Economics, where academic economists have played a considerable role in curriculum development and assessment. Business Studies has been able to reflect the concerns and interests of young people rather than adopt too theoretical a view of how businesses operate. This has allowed the subject to be accessible and motivating for young people.

The nature of GCSE Business Studies

In many respects, the nature of GCSE Business Studies is still embedded in the National Criteria developed by SEC in 1985. And yet Business Studies has been able to develop further and adapt in line with educational developments in those areas where the National Criteria were less prescriptive. As I showed in an earlier article, (Chambers, 1987) the aims, assessment objectives and content for GCSE Business Studies were clearly spelt out in the National Criteria, but advice on schemes of assessment and assessment techniques was more open.

The aims promote a broad based view of business activity, whilst in terms of content, all Business Studies syllabuses must cover 5 major headings:

1. The External Environment
2. Business Structure and Organization
3. Business Behaviour
4. People in Business
5. Aiding and Controlling Business Activity

All Business Studies syllabuses do just that, often making use of the same terminology, in terms of aims and syllabus content. 'The general conformity in content from what must have been very different regional subject groups is surprising, but perhaps reflects the influence of increased central control over the curriculum' (Chambers, 1987). The content reflects the key areas of study for the profit-making business sector, but does not allow enough scope for viewing non-profit making or public sector organizations. It takes a management or owner's perspective on business rather than an employee's or customer perspective. It does not cope adequately with the technological side of business activity, and views business from a local and national perspective rather than a European or global one. Because of the nature of this prescribed content, Business Studies teachers have found it difficult to allow pupils to explore a wider and more critical perspective on business.

Syllabus designers and examiners have found it possible to bring more flexibility to the structure of assessment than to the structure of content. A variety of assessment approaches have emerged in the Business Studies syllabuses accepted under National Criteria by SEAC.

(1) The use of differentiated and common components. This variety was initially adopted by the majority of the syllabuses under the strong guidance of the SEAC subject panel for Economics and Business Studies. It was felt that differentiated papers allowed questions to be written which were accessible to a

particular target group, and thus such papers better allowed pupils to show what they know, understand and can do. A paper set for the C–G target group would provide that group with a positive educational experience, whilst a paper set for the A–C group could then be written in a challenging way. In addition, syllabuses had two common components, a common paper with structured questions, often based on case study data, and coursework assignments allowing for differentiation by outcome. Thus examiners were able to collect information about a candidate from a range of components.

(2) *Common papers*. Only one GCSE Business Studies syllabus adopted solely common papers and coursework initially: the NEA Business Studies A syllabus. This was welcomed by teachers in that it took away the requirement of selecting which pupils to enter on the A–C route and which to enter on the C–G route (a return to the O level/CSE choice under the guise of GCSE). However, the examiners of this syllabus have found it difficult to produce two common papers equally accessible to the full ability range; the language in particular has been too difficult for the whole ability range and the examiners have had to allocate a large number of marks to each question to ensure that a full range of responses can be rewarded. This has left the candidates uncertain as to what is expected in the time and space allocated.

(3) *Extension papers*. Since 1988, both teachers and examiners have followed a steep learning curve in terms of differentiation in assessment. Changes in the way courses are being assessed for 1990 and 1991 reflect the improved confidence of GCSE examiners and teachers in setting open tasks, asking open questions and rewarding a range of responses from pupils operating at different levels. Whilst the differentiated papers were a safe starting point for examiners to ensure differentiation, experience has shown that a proportion of candidates are wrongly entered for the A–C papers, and these candidates may end up ungraded because they fall below a minimum hurdle on the higher paper. In addition, there are candidates entered for the lower general paper who might have performed at a higher level if given the opportunity. Thus a number of GCSE syllabuses are now developing a scheme of assessment comprising coursework, a common paper taken by all, and an extension paper to be taken by those who wish to aim for an A or B grade, but which would not harm candidates' results if they performed badly on that component. The common paper is likely to be targeted at the C–G levels and thus be more accessible to weaker pupils than a common paper targeted at A–G.

(4) *Modular courses*. Other syllabuses have attempted to move away from reliance upon an end of course examination in favour of using continuous assessment throughout a course divided into a number of modules. NEA Business Studies B began in 1988 with 7 modules, with some being assessed by an internally set case study and some by assignment. Experience of this course suggests that the pupils were being asked to pass through too many hoops to prove their understanding, and that teachers were being faced with a heavy load in terms of devising learning assignments and internal assessment. Pupils are now allowed to submit only 5 rather than 7 assignments. The Tameside Mode 3 Business Studies course is also modular in nature, with 3

core modules for all pupils and then the choice of two option modules from a longer list. Again, each module is internally assessed and externally moderated within the local authority and by a representative of the examination board.

Both these courses contain substantial elements where the assessment item grows out of the learning activities of the pupils; for example both have an assignment based upon an enterprise activity. The subject encourages teachers to adopt active teaching/learning strategies, and the modular framework, with less reliance on an end of course examination, is better able to allow the pupils' assessment to be based upon their normal classroom activities. In the more traditional Business Studies syllabuses, only the coursework element usually grows directly out of their classroom activities or their own research.

LEAG's Business Studies (Single Option), a course growing out of the BIS Double Option mentioned earlier, is also modular in approach, and has moved to a system of 100 per cent portfolio assessment, where pupils choose to present a portfolio of work for each module which reflects the range of learning activities they have been involved in over the two years. This is more radical than the other modular courses, where each module is assessed by one assignment or activity. Perhaps such a move will prove too radical a change. It is likely that SEAC will require a compulsory end of course, or end of module examination/assignment in GCSE syllabuses being used to assess Key Stage 4 of the National Curriculum; a 100 per cent portfolio approach would thus need to be adapted to meet this requirement. In addition, many Business Studies teachers have found it difficult to devise learning assignments and coursework assignments which allow pupils to meet the assessment objectives on which the pupils are being tested. In particular they have found it difficult to set tasks with a problem-solving rather than just a research orientation. LEAG's Business Studies (Single Option) requires just such skills throughout the course, and thus many teachers are likely to find the transition from BIS Double Option, with its emphasis on research skills, to the Single Option a demanding one.

(5) Core plus Options. A GCSE Business Studies course being introduced in 1992 by the Southern Examining Group (SEG) contains a number of interesting pointers for the future. The syllabus takes a Core plus Options structure, a form which had been contained in the original O level Business Studies course from Cambridge but which had not generally been adopted in the first round of GCSE developments (Tameside Mode 3 Business Studies being a notable exception). The core of the SEG syllabus is an integrated Business Studies core, following the lines of the National Criteria but with a reduced content element. This core makes up 80 per cent of the course, whilst the remaining 20 per cent comes from a choice of options which cover Information Technology, Commerce, Finance and Accounts, Enterprise and Modern Languages as well as a further Business Studies option. Assessment is 60 per cent by case study examination and 40 per cent by a portfolio of work done during the course. A number of features make this scheme interesting: the inclusion of the traditional business subjects of Commerce and Accounts as

options; the linking across the curriculum with Modern Languages; a stand-alone Information Technology element. This last aspect might be seen as a retrograde step, in that IT should be treated as a learning tool within business education rather than a separate bolted on element. However, the syllabus developers do emphasize that IT should be considered in relevant decision-making and communication contexts. The core plus options approach may possibly be the way in which Business Studies at GCSE will develop within the National Curriculum.

Technology and Business Studies

What is the future for GCSE Business Studies under the National Curriculum? At the time of writing, there has not been clear guidance from SEAC on the place of such subjects as Business Studies, CDT and Home Economics within Technology at Key Stage 4. Work on new National Criteria for Business Studies will not begin until Technology criteria are produced in 1991; any new GCSE Business Studies courses will need to include those elements from Key Stage 4 Technology which relate to business education, but may also include other elements from outside Technology, eg, a wider consideration of the economic and human elements of business activity. A core plus options approach may well be the form of syllabus which will fit into the cramped Key Stage 4 timetable in schools. The core might be broad based Technology with Business Studies as an option, or the core might be Business Studies with Technology elements included in the core and the options. It is certain that the number of syllabuses within the business education field at GCSE will be reduced, and that examining boards will work together to offer a suite of syllabuses common across the examining boards.

Despite this question mark over GCSE Business Studies within Key Stage 4, Technology in the National Curriculum, as described by the National Curriculum Council (DES 1990), offers opportunities to develop business understanding in pupils both at Key Stage 4 and Key Stage 3. As the Non-Statutory Guidance states:

Design and Technology is an activity which spans the curriculum, drawing on and linking a range of subjects. By creating a new subject area, work at present undertaken in art and design, business education, craft, design and technology, home economics and information technology will be co-ordinated to improve pupils' understanding of the significance of technology to the economy and the quality of life' (NCC, 1990).

Business education teachers have begun to make a contribution to the work of Technology teams in schools at Key Stage 3, and the identification of business and industry as one of the key contexts in which pupils' Technology activities take place will ensure an important and growing role for business education in Technology. Business education can provide many contexts/activities through which pupils can develop the process skills of identifying needs and opportunities, generating designs, planning and making and evaluating, and teachers of business education have become familiar with developing and assessing such activities.

Within the programmes of study for Technology, there is a strong business element. For example:

At Key Stage 3, pupils should be taught to:
- consider the influence of advertising on consumers
- identify markets for goods and services and recognize local variations in demand
- prepare a business plan, including a cash forecast and budget, and monitor performance against it
- understand how market research can be used to measure user needs and market potential
- calculate costs and make decisions on price
- recognize the relationship between price, cost, income and competition in the market for goods and services.

At Key Stage 4, pupils should be taught to:
- develop a product and how to market, promote and sell it
- recognize and take into account in their designing that people can be an element in the system
- review the ways in which market research can be used to evaluate user requirements and market potential
- know that external influences such as the level of economic development, government policy, international agencies, have effects on business activity
- measure developments against budget, evaluate variations and decide which are significant
- develop effective pricing, promotion and distribution

There are some challenging concepts here for both 11–14-year-olds and the 14–16 age group, and it will be important for business education specialists, working with others in the Technology team, to find ways of making such ideas realistic and approachable in the Technology curriculum. At present, many 16-year-olds find cash forecasting and budgeting difficult. Such concepts, however, will not occur in isolation. Good technology will involve pupils pursuing open tasks which will place the concept within a thematic context. Two examples are shown in the NCC's Non-Statutory Guidance, Designing and Making Games and Products and Packaging, which allow the application of a wide range of business skills and concepts. Thus pupils should be developing business understanding through Technology activities.

Thus important business ideas are embedded in National Curriculum Technology, ensuring that pupils from 5 to 16 will have the opportunity to explore economic and business contexts. Technology does not just attempt to promote a narrow view of business activity; it is concerned that pupils are given the opportunity to examine the social, economic, moral and environmental impact of technology activity and this should include all activities that focus upon business and industry. This should encourage business education teachers to develop in their pupils a critical and balanced view of business and industry by encouraging them to review the activities in which they are involved. In addition, business education specialists will now be working in a wider range of contexts than usual, including the home, leisure and the community. Thus their pupils must be encouraged to look at a wider range of perspectives than just the manager/owner's; the individual, the council, the family, the community will all need to be considered when such contexts are investigated.

There is uncertainty about a stand-alone GCSE Business Studies in Key Stage 4 of the National Curriculum; but there is ample opportunity in Technology for the learning experiences, key concepts and assessment approaches that have proved motivating to pupils in business education to be extended and developed. It might be best in the long run if stand-alone Business Studies does not continue after 1995; business education for all through Technology might be a better route.

References

Chambers, I (1987) 'Business Studies at GCSE', *Economics* 23, 3, 71–6.
DES (1990) *Technology in the National Curriculum.* HMSO, London.
Goodson, I (1987) *School Subjects and Curriculum Change.* Falmer Press, London
NCC (1990) *Technology. Non Statutory Guidance – Design & Technology Capability.* National Curriculum Council, York.
Taylor, A (1988) 'Economic awareness through GCSE Business Studies', in Dunnill, R and Hodkinson, S (eds) *Teaching Economic Awareness.* Heinemann, London, pp. 84–9.
Wiener, MJ (1981) *English Culture and the Decline of the Industrial Spirit 1850–1980.* Pelican, London, p. 132.

12 GCSE Coursework

David Lines

Why coursework?

In business education, the idea of coursework is far from new. The UCLES' Advanced and Ordinary levels, BTEC, the British Industrial Society syllabus, and some mode 2 and mode 3 GCSE examinations have always contained coursework. There are good educational reasons for this.

Coursework reveals skills which are not necessarily tested through conventional examination papers. Continuous assessment enhances the learning process since it requires a consistency of effort. Given effective moderation, overall assessment can be improved to give a fairer indication of a student's performance over a two-year course. Tasks can be set which are more appropriate to individual needs. Other non-subject-specific skills can be encouraged. These include communication and the development of a sense of exploration and discovery. It allows students some release from the anxiety of formal written examinations, anxiety which often causes them to perform at a standard well below their best. Some students are disadvantaged in formal examinations by social, cultural or language difficulties which can be offset by coursework. Open ended tasks remove the time constraint imposed by formal examinations, thereby also removing the potentially disastrous consequences of following 'blind alleys', or the panic engendered by, say, mathematical manipulations requiring insight as well as technical knowledge. Teaching styles can be beneficially affected. Coursework encourages a more student-centred approach. Both teachers and students can feel some release from the requirement of 'fact accumulation', so prevalent in GCE Ordinary level examinations. Teachers feel more involved with, and have a greater influence over their pupils' overall performances. It encourages links between school and the local community. Many people feel that formal examinations do not reflect the requirements of the outside world, where cooperation as much as competition is a key to success. Properly managed, coursework encourages such cooperation.

All this is not to say that coursework has been greeted with universal acclaim, and it is clear from many reports that the highly laudable objectives outlined above have by no means been reached by all. The purpose of this chapter is to encourage the achievement of that goal, by suggesting working strategies, as well as by defining the precise requirements of the GCSE Examination Groups themselves.

Setting the assignments

In order to coax out the skills[1] which may be revealed by coursework, the design of the assignment becomes very important.

It should involve central Business Studies skills

Decision making and problem solving are central to Business Studies, and therefore any assignment should encourage such approaches. Setting the piece of work in the form of a question will probably help with this.

Students should also be encouraged to use the language of the discipline wherever possible. By so doing there are bound to be positive benefits in the final examination papers as well. Explaining the meaning of a term is clearly a great deal easier if it has already been used within coursework than if it has simply been learned by rote.

Another important aspect of the study of business is its integrated nature. Assignments should reflect this integration.

The work should have a clear structure

It may be necessary to suggest headings for the students to follow, such as:

- the aims of the assignment
- the collection of data relevant to the aims
- the application of the data to the aims
- conclusions, recommendations and evaluation.

Clearly, these headings would have to be couched in terms more appropriate to the age and ability ranges of the young people involved.

The work should involve activities outside the classroom

Field research is an important part of coursework. Although such research can be confined to the school's grounds, it will lack the reality found within the business community. Local issues with which the students are familiar often provide an excellent launch pad. Whilst such an issue may arise at a point in the course which is unexpected, such an opportunity should not be wasted, since there is clear evidence that immediacy and relevance are important contributory factors in determining the relative success of assignments (SEAC, 1989a).

Despite clear statements that coursework should not become a bolt-on to normal classwork (DES, 1987; SEAC, 1989b), it is clear that this has happened in a number of cases. The dangers of this approach are clear: the students may become over-loaded; they may get the impression that coursework is some-how separate from the Business Studies that they are learning in class; teachers may find themselves 'creating' work, both for themselves and their students which is unnecessary, and possibly irrelevant.

The work should enable 'unconventional' approaches to be adopted

While a multidisciplinary approach to coursework may be unrealistic for many schools, it should certainly not be beyond the scope of the average Business Studies department to encourage the use of different media. It has been disap-pointing that the majority of assignments have been presented very convention-ally, in written form, despite exhortations from various sources to be creative (SEAC, 1989b, p. 26). After all, a multi-media approach will inevitably involve students working in groups, and this too has educational spin-offs which are themselves rapidly being translated into assessment objectives.[2] Although it is necessary for the contribution of individuals to be identified for assessment purposes, this should not act as a barrier to this type of approach, especially since so much work is done in classrooms in groups (Ison, 1989).

Students should report their findings to the class

It is unfortunate that a great deal of coursework is written by pupils in isola-tion. In many cases they spend considerable time accumulating knowledge of the business world, but then often do not have the opportunity to share that understanding with the rest of the class. In a way this is another aspect of the 'bolt-on' syndrome mentioned earlier. It is much more likely that coursework will be seen as an integral part of the learning experience if everyone can par-ticipate in the experiences of others. Such an approach might appear to be too time consuming, but like feed-back from case studies or simulations, it is never wasted time.

The length of the assignment is important

Although the examination groups sometimes set the number of words as indi-cators of likely length, these limits are not absolute. In the words of the Chief Examiners for business studies:

Moderators' experiences of the first GCSE allowed them to identify certain successful coursework tasks, as those which: . . . were of an appropriate length to meet the needs of con-tent, relevance and quality rather than a prescribed number of words (SEAC, 1989, p. 26).

Organizing assignments

One of the prime educational objectives of coursework is to teach young people that they need to organize both themselves and their work if they want to suc-ceed. This organization involves coordinating their time so that assignments from different subject areas do not clash, and for that it is reasonable to expect help from school management (SEC, 1988, pp. 3, 6, 12, 20). Some institutions have abandoned traditional homework diaries and replaced them with 'whole year planners', which include leisure activities both within and outside school as well as work, while others have developed 'Records of Achievement' booklets with the same intention (SEC, 1988, p. 36). Whatever the technique, pupils must be encouraged to set achievable targets. This is especially true of the most conscientious and able who often find themselves under enormous pressure, which cannot be either healthy or desirable.

At a basic level of organization, there are the headings mentioned above to help students structure their material, but it may well be that some time could usefully be spent in helping them with the basic techniques of research, such as those outlined below.

The questionnaire

Rumours abound that supermarket managers have been seen patrolling outside their stores with loaded shotguns waiting to ambush the next bunch of GCSE Business Studies students seen with clipboards. They have simply had enough of surveys of shopping habits! Whether these rumours are true or not, it does seem that somewhat unimaginative tasks have often been set with the objective of gathering primary data.

Questionnaires are undoubtedly an excellent way to collect such data, but it is necessary to construct them in a fairly scientific way or else the results can be meaningless.[3] The students need to decide a sample frame, perhaps undertake a pilot survey, and justify the methods used. Obviously, these points must be put across at an appropriate level, but by adding rigour, the students will be persuaded that there is more to market research than asking any question of anyone who happens to come along at any one moment.

Pie charts, etc

It does seem, all too often, that pie charts are compulsory in any piece of Business Studies coursework. In themselves they are fine, but they should not be the only means of presentation, and they should only be used when they are most appropriate.

Apart from pie charts, other ways of summarizing information include:

- Tables
- Line graphs
- Multiple line graphs
- Bar charts/multiple bar charts
- Diagrams
- Photographs
- Maps

Each of these can be used in particular circumstances as appropriate (Ison 1989, p. 22).

Presentation

Although presentation is not itself assessed, it is apparent that a piece of coursework which is neatly presented exhibits higher levels of communication skills than one which is not. Since such a skill is central to Business Studies, it is an important area for students to consider.

Equally, Information Technology is important in much of business, and so it is only right that it is incorporated in Business Studies teaching as much as possible. Clearly, word processing has advantages, not just in the neatness of presentation but also in its organization.

Other strands within IT offer potential benefits as well. Databases on the local community can be developed over time, which would offer the double benefits of desk and field research. Material from the database could be interrogated and inserted into the piece of coursework as appropriate, thereby revealing other evaluative skills.[4]

It is also a good idea to encourage students to insert acknowledgements and a bibliography into their work. The latter can have a beneficial impact, if only in persuading the student that desk research is required even when the emphasis is clearly on fieldwork.

Well organized assignments will improve the examination performance of young people, as well as enhancing their educational experiences. Nevertheless it is necessary to be quite clear as to what the examination groups require for success, and it is to that aspect that we now turn.

The Examination groups' requirements

Group	No. of assignments	% total marks
LEAG	2	20
MEG	3	30
NEA	1–3	30
NISEC	2	30
SEG	3	30
WJEC	2–4	30

This table represents only what may be termed the 'mainstream' Business Studies syllabuses. Some Groups offer alternatives.[5]

GCSE courses and requirements are continuously changing. It is always wise to refer to the most recent syllabus booklet.

London and East Anglian Group

Each year the Group prescribes six assignments, from which two are selected. They are based on local studies/surveys and may be drawn from any section of the syllabus. The assignment should be around 800–1000 words in length and is expected to show some evidence of selection, interpretation and analysis.

Midland Examining Group

The Group requires three assignments, each of which should come from different areas of the syllabus, and must be no more than 1500 words. As a general guide, each assignment should consist of 10 hours of work and should be related to a business situation or to the decision a business has to make.

Northern Examining Association

It is possible to submit one, two or three assignments into a coursework folder. If one, it must be no more than 3000 words, if two, they must be no more than 1500 words each, and if three, then not more than 1000 words. The word limits are only approximate guides.

Northern Ireland Schools Examinations Council

Two assignments should be submitted, selected from different areas of the syllabus. They should be related to a business situation or decision and should show research outside the classroom, preferably in the local community.

Southern Examining Group

The Group requires three assignments, relating to a business situation or problem. It is possible to undertake more than three, and then select the best three for final submission.

Welsh Joint Education Committee

Two to four assignments should be undertaken, based on sections of the syllabus. Approximately 30 hours of student-centred activity should be involved.

Coursework marking criteria

It is perhaps ironic that although coursework is essentially a common piece of work for all the groups, the criteria for assessing each is slightly different, not only in terms of the weighting given to different skills, but also in terms of the amount of criterion referencing attempted.[6] There seems little logic in this and it is to be hoped that this can be standardized in the future (SEAC, 1989a p. 27).

While these differences exist, it is essential that candidates preparing for an examination are clearly aware of their Group's requirement. Candidates preparing for SEG, for instance, will be assessed on four main areas:

1. Use of information
2. Comprehension
3. Application
4. Evaluation

The group is quite explicit in the marks available for each of these areas, and these could be used by a teacher as a marking template. For instance, under Section 4, Evaluation, the following is stated:

Evaluation (maximum 5 marks)

Mark	Level of performance
0	No production of any results or any conclusions.
1	Little attempt made to offer reasoned judgement in a simple way by summarizing or comparing the evidence collected.
2	Some attempt to make comments and arrive at conclusions, judgements, or recommendations, but most likely at second hand. Limitations in the presentation of logical argument.
3	Clear evidence of some ability to examine critically arguments and statements to show differing opinion. Some perception and understanding in applying judgement and recommendations to the problem. Reasonable attempt to plan work in a logical manner.
4–5	Full and sensible conclusions drawn using all the relevant data. Originality and imagination shown in solutions and conclusions. Good ability to differentiate between a well supported argument and a statement of opinion. Accurate and logical presentation.

Using the marking criteria

Drawing a grid similar to the one above, photocopying it, and attaching it with the final mark to each piece of work presents several advantages.

(1) It acts as a focus for the student. If the student is aware of the areas which are to be tested, he or she is far more likely to recognize the need to cover each area in the assignment. That is not to say that each assignment will necessarily concentrate on every area, and some teachers may well make that explicit. Nevertheless, being aware that each element is part of the assessment process can only help in accumulating marks.

(2) It acts as a focus for the teacher. Coursework must be assessed in its entirety. It is a help, however, to recognize that the Examination Groups are looking for certain skills to be exercised, and marking will inevitably be eased if those skills can be identified. Moderation may also be simplified through such a system.

(3) It acts as a check on progress. Over a period, both the student and the teacher can identify strengths and weaknesses more clearly.

(4) It promotes more meaningful coursework. The very fact that, for instance, the skill of evaluation is required means that assignments of a purely descriptive nature are more likely to be avoided. In certain schools, students have been sent out on work experience, and have then written it up as a piece of Business Studies coursework. The results have largely been inappropriate simply because they described what the student did during that placement, rather than making meaningful comments about the way the business operated within a wider business context. To this end, it is desirable to put the coursework into the form of a question. By so doing, the student is forced to

make some kind of judgement; in effect evaluating (Ison and Lines, 1989, p. 6; Chambers, 1987, p. 75).

Conclusion

Coursework is here to stay; indeed its extension into the post-16 curriculum appears to be only a matter of time. Some may question the automatic assumption of its benefits, and more research is required into its impact on teaching and learning. Nonetheless, there are considerable potential benefits, and there can be little doubt that many young people, and their teachers, have gained from its introduction. Clearly the period of experimentation is still very much with us, but progress is being made, and with the help of dedicated and thoughtful teachers, it will continue.

Notes

1. For a full list of attainment targets see *Working Paper 2: Coursework Assessment in GCSE*, SEC, May 1985, pp. 2–4.
2. A number of GCSE examinations in Business Studies now contain groupwork assessment. For example LEAG's Business and Information Studies and SEG's Core Plus IT Option.
3. Many books on marketing contain information on questionnaire design, but for a straightforward and easily understood version, see *Marketing* by Martin, ET, Mitchell Beazley, 1983, pp. 20–25.
4. For an interesting and useful account of possible uses of IT within Business Studies, see Davies, P and Allison, R, 'Computer Assisted Learning Feature – Using Databases in Economics and Business Studies' in *Economics* 25, Part 2, 106, Summer 1989, pp. 73–7.
5. LEAG offers three syllabuses, the mainstream plus the BIS single and BIS double options. Both the NEA and SEG offer two. The NEA's Syllabus B is based entirely around coursework. SEG's alternative, again called Syllabus B, contains 80 per cent Business Studies plus a 20 per cent IT component. From the 1992 examination SEG will be offering a 'Core plus Options' package. The core will be 80 per cent 'straight' Business Studies, with options including IT, Commerce, British Industrial Society, and a modern foreign language. There is a Teacher's Guide available from SEG for this new course containing much of value, including a section on coursework.
6. For a more detailed discussion, see 'Assessing Business Studies Coursework' by Hunter, L, in Cullimore, D (ed), *Teaching Business Education: A Teachers' Manual*, Business Education Publishers, 1990.

References

Chambers, I (1987) 'Business Studies at GCSE', *Economics* 23, pp. 71–6, Part 3, 99.
DES (1987) *GCSE: The National Criteria*. HMSO, London.
DES (1987) *The National Criteria for Business Studies*. HMSO, London.
Ison, S and Lines, D (1989) *GCSE Coursework*. Longman, Harlow.
SEAC (1989a) *Chief Examiners Conference in Business Studies*. SEAC, London.
SEAC (1989b) *Chief Examiners Conference in Economics*. SEAC, London.
SEC (1988) *Working Paper 6: Managing GCSE Coursework in Schools*. SEC, London.

13 Modular Courses at A Level: The Peterborough Approach

Maureen Maurice and Marjorie Pirie

The questions to be addressed

What fears are conjured up in people's minds when considering a modular syllabus? What might be the implications for school, teacher and student? How is it possible to deliver an integrated subject in modular form? What implications are there for timetabling? How are students able to see the whole when it is split up into bits? Can they see the wood for the trees? Could a school be tempted to timetable specialist staff for individual modules without making provision for consultation? How does one deal with overlap of content on the one hand and the constraints of module parameters on the other? Does pupil or teacher absence have greater implications in a modular syllabus? How easy is it for pupils to become demotivated? All these are very real fears and need to be addressed.

In this chapter we set out to answer these questions in the light of our own experience in the classroom and as examiners and trainers.

Does a modular structure aid learning?

Although students may not be able to cope with absorbing the implications of the whole course, they can cope with a 'module's worth'. They can see the parameters of the module. This is an advantage for both bright and less bright students, for the brighter students can speed ahead, and the less able can get started on the bits to which they are attracted. In that way, they build on what they understand. Group work is particularly effective in this process.

Students are more motivated in their learning through short-term targets. Even if those targets are not reached, it is still a motivating factor, because their learning curve is not so deep and can be easily boosted. It is important to present the module as a series of tasks, some of which will elicit a more enthusiastic response than others. This enthusiasm within a group will motivate the less enthusiastic members. Mixed-ability learning becomes a possibility, indeed, a success.

A new module allows students to feel they have a fresh start. They may feel they have done badly or not enjoyed one module, and they can be encouraged to believe that they may enjoy a new one and perhaps improve their performance.

One of the greatest strengths of modular courses is the opportunity to give constant feedback on tasks, both throughout and at the end of the module. A common assumption is that students will be demotivated by a poor result at the end of the module; we have not found this to be so.

Modules mean deadlines. To enable students to build up confidence more quickly, they need to be set achievable target times. When they succeed and meet the deadlines – not something achieved overnight, but built up particularly during the first two modules – they feel capable of taking on responsibility for their own work. This in turn can increase their commitment to the course. However, in order for every child to have some measure of success, the teacher must ensure that deadlines are achievable. A degree of flexibility may be necessary with some students.

How is it possible to deliver an integrated subject in modular form?

The structure of the syllabus is of paramount importance. There are two main ways to structure a modular syllabus – one makes use of a foundation module and the other a core module.

A foundation module presents the breadth of the complete syllabus as an introduction on which to build and develop in-depth understanding of the rest of the course. Examples of such modules feature in the Cambridge Modular A Level and the Tameside GCSE.

A core module generally states the principal elements which need to be taught throughout the course. There is a danger of fragmentation unless the teacher identifies which of those elements need to be linked to give basic understanding of the concepts of business studies. Examples of core modules include the BIS A Level and the Shared Business Experience A Level.

Good planning and mapping of the whole course is essential. It is the teacher's responsibility to ensure that integration takes place. The student, especially at GCSE level, will not necessarily recognize the links between the concepts. The student will only work within the parameter of the module, and the teacher needs to see that module within the parameters of the subject. Using case studies allows natural integration within each module and the course.

A foundation module should encourage an holistic approach to the subject. By having an overview, students get a better idea of relationships between concepts. This can then be built upon at a later stage. Overlap between areas of the syllabus is less of a problem than with a linear course, since any revisits to an area will be with a different brief.

The Cambridge Business Studies Modular syllabus A level uses the foundation module (double weighted) to cover the breadth of the subject, which together with a research assignment comprises an A/S level. Specialist modules in the second year of the A level key into and build upon what has been taught in the double module.

What are the implications for the school, teacher and student of a modular course?

The timetable can be a particular restraint on what might be the best way to run a course. However, a good timetabler can build in the flexibility to team teach, allocate block time and a work experience element, if informed of needs in advance and if sympathetic to the philosophy of the course. If the above is not possible, then many resulting problems can be overcome by good planning and regular consultation between involved members of staff. This is especially important when the teaching of a module has to be split.

However, there are gains for both teachers and students in having more than one member of staff involved in the course: the opportunity for individual teachers to offer their own specialisms to enrich the students' learning; the encouragement and benefit afforded by gradually moving on into new areas of expertise and the resultant professional development of the teacher. It also affords the opportunity for a new teacher to take on the syllabus, for, if one of a team, it should be possible gradually to take on new modules as he/she feels able. A teacher who has sole responsibility for running the course should not find integration a problem, but a modular course is extremely demanding for the sole teacher.

If a modular course allows students to select modules, then they have control of their study in a way that does not seem to occur in other schemes. Whether chosen for special interest, expertise, or with a particular career in mind, students become motivated by being allowed that kind of discretion.

Does a modular-style syllabus lend itself to one style of teaching rather than another?

It is possible to deliver a modular syllabus in a didactic manner, but at the risk of demotivating many students. However, it would be foolish to expect that all concepts could be understood through student-centred learning. Group work is an important vehicle for learning, when the teacher is vigilant in checking that the basic concepts are understood, and is ready to correct any deficiency. Often, a talk-and-chalk lesson is the answer. Group working on case studies gives the teacher the opportunity to observe the different levels at which students are working. Individual and group skills develop naturally, thus saving time, which is of particular relevance in a modular syllabus.

Case study material obtained from newspapers, television, etc stimulates interest and learning more successfully than that available in books. Moreover, it can be particularly useful when gaps in learning have been identified by the teacher. One simple, short, tailor-made case study can be an effective remedial technique. This gives flexibility to accentuate one area more than another.

What relevance does assessment have in a modular syllabus?

A great deal! The opportunity for direct feedback from an assessment at the end of each module is of inestimable value to student and teacher.

The feedback motivates – students can see how they are succeeding, or failing, and are motivated to improve in both cases. It pinpoints any weaknesses which the student and teacher can seek to remedy. It is a reliable indicator for forecasting final grades, and gives students the opportunity to gauge suitability for further education or work. Indeed, at A Level, when students are applying for higher education, they will have actual module grades to enter on their forms, rather than just predicted grades. These grades can also be used for students going straight into jobs.

The problem of boredom can occur, however, in a syllabus where there is insufficient variety in methods of assessment. The teacher must be aware of this in the planning stages of the course. Some students respond better to one form of assessment than another, so where a syllabus offers choice, this difficulty can be easily overcome.

The heavy revision programme and timing of end-of-course examinations penalises many students. Revision is easily built into the modular programme. At the end of the course, when other linear subjects are examined, modular students benefit from having only the end-of-module assessment.

With the Cambridge Modular A level Business Studies, there is opportunity to improve grades by retaking modules, although teachers need to be aware that it is not always in the student's best interest to retake while continuing to take other modules. However, this can be a valuable option for some students and remains open to them for five years.

Those involved in writing modular syllabuses have been concerned that there could be a tendency for students to be over-assessed in comparison with those taking a linear syllabus. This needs to be borne in mind when selecting a syllabus.

Conclusion

It is our belief that our students have gained from modular courses in many ways, some of which we have mentioned in this chapter. We had thought that students might find the pressure of module deadlines a difficulty. In practice, they soon organize their workload, and find that having just one module to cope with at the end of the two years is a relief and bonus. It has also been interesting to discover that when more than one modular course is being studied, students adapt well. Group pressure keeps absence rates low, but when it does occur, the student realizes the work needs to be made up because of the module deadline.

We also believe that we have gained as teachers. Enthusiasm and a readiness to move into new areas is a common experience we have shared with our own students and colleagues with whom we have worked, or met, in different parts of the country.

A modular scheme gives more opportunity for curriculum development. New modules can be added to extend student choice, and the scheme can be flexible enough to allow for integration with other subjects, eg, three modules from Business Studies plus three modules from Technology. Cross-centre learning can become a possibility, eg, different centres offering expertise in modules. This may seem a nightmare for some timetablers; for other centres, it may be seen as a solution to the problems associated with a small Sixth Form, or departments with only one teacher.

A modular scheme does not necessarily mean more teacher involvement with assessment, but often does. Some teachers may see this as a negative factor, as it places greater demands on their time. But many teachers see this as an opportunity to work more closely with their students, and have a better understanding of the demands of the course and consequently be of more help to their students.

We are convinced that a well-structured modular syllabus provides the breadth and balance sought by teachers as educationally desirable.

14 BTEC Business Studies

Steven Blowers

Levels of BTEC awards

The Business and Technician Education Council (BTEC) is a validating body offering pre-vocational and vocational courses (for example, in business and finance) at a variety of levels (see Figure 14.1). The Foundation Programme aims to add a pre-vocational dimension to the curriculum for 14–16 year olds. Post-16, the Certificate of Pre-Vocational Education (CPVE) is a one-year course aimed at those who are vocationally uncommitted, and students may change vocational direction part-way through a course. BTEC First and National courses are aimed at those who are vocationally committed from the start of the course. Although CPVE courses often include opportunities to obtain GCSE and other qualifications, eg Royal Society of Arts (RSA), BTEC courses post-16 are designed as discrete courses and are not combined with others.

BTEC/City and Guilds Foundation Programme	For school pupils in years 10 and 11, usually associated with a programme of GCSEs
BTEC/City and Guilds Certificate of Pre-vocational Education (CPVE)	National Vocational Qualification (NVQ) Level 1
BTEC First Awards	NVQ Level 2
BTEC National Awards	Equivalent to: NVQ Level 3 2 or 3 A Levels, depending on level of attainment achieved

Figure 14.1 *Levels of awards*

CPVE courses have developed strongly in schools, in particular in the vocational area of Business Administration, and in many instances links have been fostered between the secondary and further education (FE) sectors. BTEC First Courses have only been available to students in the past through FE colleges, and although National courses have been introduced successfully in some schools, these have also predominately been available through the FE sector. From September 1991, however, it will be possible for schools and Sixth Form colleges to offer BTEC First courses (subject to a satisfactory application for approval to run a course), and First and National courses are likely to be offered more widely in the future, often involving links between the secondary and FE sectors.

BTEC First and National Certificates are designed for part-time students (to complement experience from employment), and BTEC First and National Diplomas are designed for students in full-time education. It is not intended, therefore, that students in full-time education undertake certificate courses coupled with, for example, a programme of GCSEs or A–A/S levels, as the experience from employment would be missing.

BTEC specify the number of hours of formal learning support which First and National courses require, with units (modules) for certificate students requiring less support, as learning is complemented by work-based experience. First Certificate courses require 300 hours in total, First Diplomas 720 hours, National Certificate courses 750 hours and National Diplomas 1485 hours. This usually means that First courses are completed in one year and National courses in two years. Certificate courses are usually offered to adults in work on a day-release basis or can be taken in the evenings (usually two per week).

For all courses post-16, BTEC are seeking or have received accreditation from the National Council for Vocational Qualifications (NCVQ). These courses include: CPVE preparatory modules at National Vocational Qualification (NVQ) Level 1, BTEC First Awards at Level 2, and BTEC National Awards at Level 3. Students following courses will be assessed on a range of NVQ (work-based competences) and other BTEC outcomes (eg, a range of skills) and will achieve a BTEC Award (eg, a BTEC First Diploma) with NVQ accreditation (eg, at Level 2).

Programmes available

Courses leading to BTEC qualifications aim to provide a broad educational foundation which will equip students for a range of careers in a rapidly changing world. It is expected that courses will be both intellectually challenging and designed to assist students to cope with all aspects of the work environment (BTEC, 1985, 1986).

Schools and colleges wishing to offer BTEC courses are required to submit an application to BTEC for approval to run a course. Once approval has been obtained, a moderator will be appointed, whose responsibility it is to work with course teams to ensure course delivery in line with the approved submission and BTEC's overall philosophy. The aim of this external moderation is to ensure quality control in the provision of all BTEC courses.

BTEC courses are based on a philosophy which includes:

- modular structures
- involving local employers in the planning, development and evaluation of courses

- a course team (of teaching staff), whose members have a variety of appropriate business experiences, responsible for planning and delivering a course
- a student-centred approach to course delivery
- the use of assignments and case studies
- integration of learning experiences across units/modules when appropriate
- the development of a range of business related and personal skills as an integral part of the learning experience
- work, vocational and/or community experience for all students
- continuous assessment (a part of this process for First and National Awards is an end of year assessment).

Foundation programmes

As a guide, a pupil may follow a foundation programme as an alternative to two GCSEs during years 10 and 11 at school (about 20 per cent of curriculum time). The Joint Board's (BTEC and City and Guilds) regulations expect a pupil to complete a minimum of 200 hours' work in a two-year programme, studying at least two modules. The programme is intended, however, to integrate vocational elements of the curriculum with the general education requirements of the National Curriculum. This intention to integrate is best achieved through a programme which combines appropriate elements of GCSE courses and the modules undertaken by a pupil, rather than through a stand-alone programme viewed as an unrelated alternative to GCSEs. The programme is aimed at pupils of all abilities and should not be viewed as being aimed solely at the less able.

A school's programme is based on the modular concept, designed by the Joint Board, which involves four themes and four contexts. Each theme can be studied in each context, giving a total of sixteen modules from which to choose (see Figure 14.2). Pupils work on a number of active learning opportunities (case studies) and these provide the basis for assessment. A pupil's progress is identified and recorded on a profile.

Themes	Contexts
Arts and design	Business administration and distribution
Money	Production and technical services
People	Self and the environment
Technology	Services to people, eg, health care

Figure 14.2 *Foundation programme themes and contexts*

There is clearly much scope here for business education teachers to be involved with others in the planning and delivery of a foundation programme. For example, working with Home Economics teachers, case study material could be prepared for use in a module looking at budgeting (money) and food preparation, in the context of deciding between the advantages of different types of catering outlets (services to people). This could form the basis of activities involving pupils in GCSE courses in Business Studies and Home Economics, offering an opportunity to integrate elements of a foundation programme with some GCSE work.

A range of skills, including collecting, analysing and presenting information, decision-making and interpersonal skills are required to be developed. These should be integrated in the main learning programme, eg, working in groups, pupils collect information (costs) on materials (food) and production (food preparation), decide which catering outlet (fast food v. at table) offers the most opportunity (cost v. quality/revenue v. job satisfaction).

As the requirements of the NCVQ became clearer, the challenge will be to identify how Foundation Programmes can offer opportunities to achieve competences at NVQ Level 1 and above, and to ensure that this prior learning is accredited, giving students a head start when beginning any new course post-16.

The Certificate of Pre-vocational Education

The availability of BTEC First courses in schools from September 1991 raises a question mark over the future of the CPVE. CPVE programmes have worked well when all non-A-A/S level year 12 (first year Sixth) pupils in a school have been involved, often combining a number of GCSEs through the additional studies element and/or through schemes which integrate a limited number of GCSE subjects (eg, in Business Studies, English and Mathematics) with the vocational and core elements of the course. Students have often decided upon a vocational area in which to specialize at 16, and developments in the future are increasingly likely to see BTEC First courses replace the CPVE, as NVQ Level 2 targets can be reached by the more able and motivated student. There will be a loss of flexibility, in that a student will be less able to switch vocational areas having started a course, but few CPVE schemes have been able to develop this opportunity successfully to any great extent. The aim of the Foundation Programme, to add a pre-vocational dimension to the curriculum for 14–16 year olds, may therefore be seen as more desirable in the future.

There has been some debate as to whether A-A/S level students should undertake a two year CPVE programme during their course of study. The educational merits of students at the equivalent of NVQ Level 3 following a programme over two years, designed for NVQ Level 1 students over one year, should be seriously questioned. Schemes which combine BTEC National courses (NVQ Level 3) and A-A/S levels are being developed, and would be more appropriate (see below).

Development of BTEC First courses in schools

Of most interest to schools will be the BTEC First course in Business and

Finance, which currently offers students a core of study based around a unit entitled Working in Organizations, three interdisciplinary themes (money, technology and change) and a number of business-related and personal skills (including information gathering, identifying and tackling problems and using information technology). In addition, Certificate students have to undertake a further two option units, and Diploma students a further five. These can be selected from a pool of standard BTEC option units including, for example, finance, information processing, secretarial/office options (eg, word processing) and units related to distribution (eg, consumer legislation). The core is given a unit value equal to three option units.

There are no formal entry requirements for students, but they must have achieved 'a standard of literacy and numeracy and accompanying level of education and competence sufficient to enable [them] to benefit from and succeed on the course' (BTEC, 1986). No overall pass or grade is awarded on completion of the course. Instead, the level of attainment achieved by a student in each separately assessed part (units and skills) of the course is graded distinction, merit, pass or fail.

The BTEC First Award in Business and Finance is being piloted in a form with NVQ Level 2 accreditation, and it should be generally available in this form from September 1991. This allows schemes to be devised which permit students limited access to GCSE and other (eg, recreation) courses, and will include a greater emphasis on students acquiring competences in the work place. Also of interest to business education teachers is the development of a course at this level in Information Technology applications. It will be interesting to see whether it will be possible to combine elements of this with the Business and Finance or other first courses, to allow students to choose between vocational areas part way through their course.

BTEC National in Business and Finance

Of all BTEC courses at National Level, Business and Finance is the most popular, taken by over 50 per cent of all National level students. Other courses at this level which might also be of interest to business education teachers include:

- Distribution Studies
- Hotel Catering and Leisure Services
- Public Administration
- Information Technology (IT) Applications.

BTEC has established the entry requirements which students must achieve to gain access to this level of course. In addition to being able to 'satisfy the [school or college] providing the course that [their] level of competence in English language and numeracy is sufficient to enable [them] to understand and progress satisfactorily on the course' (BTEC, 1985), a student must have obtained one of the following:

- a BTEC First Certificate or Diploma
- a CPVE with an appropriate profile
- 4 GCSEs at grades A, B or C.

One of the successes of the CPVE has been the opportunity courses have offered students to achieve a level on their profile sufficient to gain entry to BTEC courses at National level, without the necessity of achieving four GCSEs at grades A, B or C. It is important that this level is defined at the beginning of a CPVE course, and made available to students, in order to give them a target for which to aim.

A programme must be based around the three elements offered by BTEC: the core element (compulsory units), the additional element (option units) and a business-related skills element. Skills are required to be developed progressively within and across units, as are three interdisciplinary themes (money, technology and change). Certificate courses are not required to offer as many option units in the additional element as are required for diploma courses (see Figure 14.3). Business related skills (including information gathering, identifying and tackling problems and information processing) have a total unit value equivalence of 2.0, core units 1.5 each and most option units 1.0 each. The minimum total unit value equivalence a student must achieve is 12.5 for a Certificate to be awarded and 16.5 for a Diploma. Option units include, for example, advertising, marketing, information processing, accounting, elements of banking, business law, secretarial units (eg, keyboarding and its applications) and units related to distribution and travel and tourism. It is also possible to include units in modern languages.

As with BTEC First awards, no overall pass or grade is awarded on completion of the course. Instead, the level of attainment achieved by a student in each separately assessed part (core and option units and business related skills) of the course is graded distinction, merit, pass or fail.

Combined schemes in 'academic' and 'vocational' BTEC courses

Genuine credit transfer between academic and vocational courses, or some form of 'baccalaureate' combining individual subjects and modules/units, does not yet exist. The desirability of combining these two approaches, to widen a student's educational experience and to cater for more than just the academically able, is currently being discussed. Until more formal progress has been made, there is much which teachers in business education can do to move in this direction.

Foundation programmes can include genuinely integrated learning experiences, with assessed outcomes both in terms of GCSE and Joint Board modules. CPVE schemes have demonstrated that integrated learning experiences can also lead to a variety of outcomes, for example:

- work completed for the preparatory module in Enterprise Skills can also prepare students for GCSEs in Business Studies and Mathematics

	Year 1	Year 2
Core units	Business related skills Finance People in Organizations 1 The Organization in its Environment 1	Business related skills People in Organizations 2 The Organization in its Environment 2
Additional option units		
Certificate	1 unit	2 units
Diploma	3 units	4 units

Figure 14.3 *BTEC National units for Business and Finance*

- the development of IT skills can be assessed as a part of the CPVE profile (including the preparatory module in Data Handling), or as part of an RSA single subject award (eg, word processing) or it may prepare students for a GCSE in Business Studies with an option in IT (eg, LEAG syllabus B).

The development of BTEC First courses with NVQ accreditation should offer an opportunity to develop some common learning experiences which aim to prepare students for a variety of assessable outcomes, eg, GCSE, NVQ and BTEC.

This approach has been extended to BTEC National courses in Business and Finance and A-A/S Levels. BTEC are aiming to pilot a scheme from September 1991, which is based on the same principle, that from a common learning experience it is possible to achieve a variety of assessable outcomes. The scheme offers students an integrated first year programme, which combines elements of the BTEC National Diploma with A/AS Levels in, for example, Business Studies and Sociology. In the second year, students choose between completing a programme of 3 A Levels/2 A Levels and 2 AS Levels or completing the BTEC National Diploma in Business and Finance. An interesting feature of the scheme in the first year is an element for all students which includes developing IT and foreign language skills and a period of work/vocational experience. The choice between the academic or vocational path is, therefore, delayed for one year and can be made on the basis of student experience. Opportunity is provided for all students to develop a range of skills useful to further study and/or employment.

Effective delivery of BTEC courses

BTEC courses need to be delivered in line with the Board's stated guidelines on aims, entry requirements, course design and structure, course implementation (including cross-curricular themes and skills), assessment and course approval and moderation. These vary according to the level and title of the course chosen. Schools and colleges are not free to offer courses without

BTEC's approval, and are subject to the Board's on-going moderation procedures and requirements (which can be quite extensive). Application forms are
available from BTEC.

The key points which underpin BTEC's overall philosophy, listed above,
provide a useful checklist for establishments considering BTEC courses. The
involvement of local employers during the design (what is the relationship
between the units/modules offered and the pattern of local employment?) and
running of the course is essential. Case studies and assignments based on
local examples, made realistic by employer involvement, should be an essential feature of any BTEC course. Employers can also be involved in the
assessment of students' work, for example, assisting in grading the presentation of a group's business plan. Women in business and business people from
ethnic minority groups can provide positive role models for students which
challenge traditional perceptions. Businesses need not only be large private
sector companies, but should also include many other examples (eg, from the
voluntary sector, the self employed, cooperatives, the public sector) from the
primary and manufacturing as well as service sectors of the economy.

Integration is the key to the delivery of all BTEC courses. Skills and
themes cannot be delivered in isolation, and genuinely need to be developed
throughout a course. The relationship between units needs to be made clear.
For example, elements of accounting will appear in many units, and can effectively be used to develop IT skills (eg, spreadsheets). This requires a well
planned and systematic approach to course design and the development of
materials. Unnecessary duplication should be avoided, and it should be possible
to identify when opportunities are available to students progressively to develop
and practise their skills throughout a course.

An effective method of integrating across units and providing a framework
in which skills and themes can be developed is to base learning experiences
across a whole course on a series of contexts which could in turn be linked to a
vocational experience, for example, the Young Enterprise (YE) scheme (see
Figure 14.4). Students can be assessed through a series of integrated assignments, one for each context. It is very helpful to First and National level students
if grade criteria (a clear description of what a student needs to do in order to
achieve each grade possible) are included with assignments which are to be
assessed. Skills and competences should similarly be specified; what a student
needs to do in the *context* of the work they are undertaking (not simply a
repeat of the skill or competence statement from the BTEC booklet) should
be clearly spelt out.

Teaching and learning should be student-centred. The use of case studies,
open ended assignments, problem-solving situations, group work, visits, work
simulation and role play should be included in the teaching techniques
employed. This will require (particularly important in schools) the establishment of specialist facilities which allow group work (eg, business presentations) to take place and give students access to an appropriate range of
resources (eg, periodicals, newspapers, specialist and reference books, appropriate video and tape materials, computers and telephone, including Prestel

Theme for unit teaching and assessment (weeks)	Young Enterprise activity based in local firm, half-day per week
Induction (2)	Visit to firm
Starting a business (4)	Students set up a YE company
Surviving in the market place (4)	Trading begins
Business organization and management (4)	Development of company structure
Public sector business activity (4)	Comparison of private/public sector businesses
Work experience: Preparation (1) Placement (3) De-brief (1)	Experience of different types of work
Employment and unemployment (4)	Job roles, winding-up the company
Problem-solving and decision-making in business (7)	Review of YE business; for First and National courses this could provide the context for end of year assessments

Figure 14.4 *Example framework for a BTEC course over one year*

services). BTEC specify a minimum level of resources for some units. For example, at National level, Information Processing requires one business computer for every two students. Teaching staff are also required to have had appropriate business experience. One way of achieving up-to-date experience, especially for the more specialized units, (advertising, for example), is for the members of a course team to undertake work experience themselves. This can also establish useful contacts between a school/college and local firms and provide the basis for writing case study and assignment materials.

BTEC courses in Business Studies have proved to be successful when well planned and delivered. Students can be highly motivated by an approach which is centred on the learner, more vocational, and continually assessed or profiled. Courses can be interesting and satisfying to teach, and BTEC's external moderation, when functioning well, serves as a source of support and advice, as well as an essential means of quality control. There are many opportunities and challenges ahead for business educationalists in curriculum development, none more so than the moves in education post–16 towards credit transfer between vocational and academic courses, the accreditation of prior learning and the development of a range of core skills for all students (NCC, 1990).

References

BTEC (1985) *BTEC National Courses. Business and Finance. Distribution and Public Administration.* Guidelines, BTEC, London.

BTEC (1986) *BTEC First Courses. Business and Finance and Distribution.* Guidelines, BTEC, London.
NCC (1990) *Core Skills 16–19.* National Curriculum Council, York.

SECTION 3: RESOURCES AND MISCELLANEOUS INFORMATION

15 Simulations for Economics and Business Education

David Whitehead

This annotated bibliography of published simulations excludes all computer-aided exercises, not because they lack value, but for reasons of space. For the same reason, we omit discussion of how to use simulations. For the best advice in this field, turn to any of the publications by Ken Jones on their use, such as that referred to in the list of sources.

In order to decide which simulations might be worth using, refer to the index at the end of the chapter, which lists appropriate simulations for teaching specific concepts ot topics. The numbers after each title refer to the source of simulations, listed after the index.

1. *The Aims of Firms* – Alain Anderton (17)
Each group is a board of directors of a drug company, deciding which of three drugs to develop and market. Illustrates differences between private and social costs and benefits, commercial and the public interest.

2. *Assembly Line* – Dennis C Dobbs, Carol G Goodell, and Robert F Hill (1, p. 67)
Provides the learner with a dramatic and dynamic model of a mass production system. It leads to an understanding of how mass production methods have increased productivity and reduced units costs. It also provides insights into the social changes that lead to the creation of new jobs, the disappearance of old jobs, and the sharp increase in the use of natural resources. It provides players with an opportunity to simulate many assembly line working conditions. The assembly line produces a paper cut-out car. It is also possible to have one individual assembling the car independently, to offer contrasts between the two systems.

3. *Auction* – Sarah Wilkinson (2, p. 72)
This simulated auction aims to demonstrate that price is market-determined. It allows students to experience market forces in operation. Consumer surplus and the effects of inequality of income distribution are demonstrated.

4. *Balance of Payments Problem* – John Wolinski (1, p. 233)
This presents the dilemma facing a government whose only economic consideration (in the model) is to retain a favourable balance of payments and, at the same time, remain sufficiently popular to stay in power. Each group repre-

sents the government of a country, and has to choose from 35 possible policies. The controller has a table listing the balance of payments effect of each policy, together with its political impact. Twelve random events may be introduced, if so desired.

5. *Banks and the Creation of Money* – Alain Anderton (1, p. 207)
Shows how banks can create money. It may also promote discussion about the oligopolistic nature of British banking. Each player is a director of one of four banks, each of which has to decide what interest to pay on deposits and charge for loans, and how many branches to set up.

6. *Bank Loan* (18)
Students are bank managers deciding on whether to grant loans to a variety of potential borrowers. Raises questions of liquidity, solvency and collateral security.

7. *Barsetshire* – Paul Reynolds (3, p. 15.1)
Based on a study of the implications of changes in population, students identify the various policy choices which a local authority must make when faced with a change in its population profile. Involves interpretation of data supplied, and cost-benefit analysis.

8. *Barter* – David R Butler (1, p. 75)
In this simulation, students have to barter pencils and rulers, to illustrate the problems of fixed exchange rates and indivisibility. Then erasers are introduced into the market, and the problem of a double coincidence of wants is illustrated.

9. *Bildex: Conflicts over Chemical Pollution* – 4 Ian Marcousé (3, p. 11.1)
A failing chemical company has launched a crucial new product which could save it, and many jobs, in the North East, yet the factory's high pollution emissions threaten workers and residents. If they publicise this, sales may suffer. Students are divided into union members, residents, and management, and have to decide whether environmental safety ot jobs take precedence. Aims to stimulate thought on the potential conflict between profit and social responsibilities, how goals may conflict, and especially to demonstrate conflicts of interest within society other than the stereotypical 'bosses against workers'.

10. *The Bradford Game* (8)
Students represent companies producing paper notebooks. Each group is given the same raw materials, and has to organize the production process and try to maximize profits. Concepts include division of labour, quality control, accounts, assembly line.

11. *Can we save Logo Motors* – Ken Jones (13)
The middle management of four organizations: Logo Motors, a firm of economic consultants, a union and a government ministry consider this lame-duck company, and what should be done about it. Skills include analysing economic data, planning, negotiating and decision-making.

12. *Capital City* (8)
This exercise on public finance introduces local government, and presents the dilemmas facing administrators, as well as providing insights into committee work and decision making.

13. *Capitalist* - Alain Anderton (1, p. 167)
Shows the effects of increasing returns to scale in an industry. Billshire is starting to develop, and is about to undergo an agricultural revolution due to newly discovered techniques. Each team represents a farming family, which starts off with one of twenty-five plots of land in Billshire, one unit of labour and capital, and some money. The winning team is that with the most assets at the end of play.

14. *Collective Bargaining* - Stuart Luker (2, p. 188)
A standard collective bargaining simulation, with briefing notes for employers' and union's negotiators.

15. *Community Expenditure* (16)
Students consider economic criteria in making environmental, social and political judgements to implement proposed local spending cuts.

16. *Deadlines* (4)
Simulation for understanding media bias about the Third World, in particular how newspapers cover stories from other countries.

17. *Division of Labour* - Alain Anderton (17)
Teams of four workers produce eight birthday cards as efficiently as possible, given quality control. Also raises question of job satisfaction.

18. *The Economy of Oltenia* - Gordon Hewitt (1, p. 221)
Each participant has to provide the Chancellor with answers to a letter from the PM, concerning next year's level of National Income, whether this will result in a labour shortage or unemployment, and if the latter, whether to increase government expenditure or reduce taxation. Demonstrates clearly the use of the national income formula, budget and trade deficits, and the multiplier.

19. *Essex Raspberry Zooglebar Co. Ltd* - Kevin Tinsley (2, p. 98)
A management/trade union simulation, concerning conditions of work, and possible employer negligence.

20. *Export Decisions and the Exchange Rate* - Ann Cotterrell (7, 24. 4.128)
Student groups decide whether to export a consignment of golf trollies to Italy and shortbread to Canada. The aim is to encourage the understanding of the effects of exchange rate changes and the use of forward rates.

21. *Fares Fare* - Kevin Butters and Chris Riley (3, p. 2.1)
Four groups of students act the roles of management consultants, a trade union working party, various townspeople and the local authority transport committee. They consider policy recommendations concerning the subsidized bus service. Covers the concepts of free markets, government intervention, opportunity costs and subsidies.

22. *Farmer* - Alain Anderton (1, p. 168)
Wheat farmers are presented with a production matrix, and must decide how much to produce, given the price of capital and labour and the unit price of wheat. The object is to reinforce the idea that for profit maximization, firms will aim to produce where $MC = MR$.

23. *The Farming Game* (4 or 5)
This is a revised version of *The Poverty Game*. Participants are subsistence

farmers in the Savannah region of Africa. Dice, chance and disease cards to great extent control their fate.

24. *Five Simple Business Games* (8)
Gorgeous Gateaux, Fresh Oven Pies and Dart Aviation aim to help students understand how a business works; The Island Game and The Republic Game indicate how industry creates wealth. Also available computerized.

25. *Foreign Exchange* – Dan Moynihan and Brian Titley (3, p. 13.1)
Designed to give students an insight into the interdependence of trading nations in the world economy. Students try to predict movements in exchange rates in order to secure a supply of materials for their company at the lowest possible cost. Concepts include foreign exchange rates, demand and supply of foreign currency, and speculation.

26. *Games Theory Game* – Alain Anderton (1, p. 165)
This game allows students to experience the sort of situation which games theory tries to explain, so that they can discuss optimal strategies, and their relevance to the theory of the firm. Students take decisions for two firms, from a zero sum matrix, and calculate profits depending on their decision in relation to that taken by their competitor.

27. *The Grain Drain* (4)
A board game based on the politics of food, illustrating the problems faced by many Third World countries in buying grain and food on the world market.

28. *Greater Dhaka Power Plant* (14)
Based on an actual project funded by the British government, it shows the way a particular aid project affected different social groups, demonstrating who benefited from it. Encourages discussion about effective aid and priorities in development.

29. *Home-made or Trade?* – Charles Gunningham (3, p. 7.1)
Students trade small cut-out coloured cards of varying shapes, and observe and record what happens. First, autarky prevails. Then, free world trade is allowed. Concepts to be derived include export/import, balance of trade, surplus/deficit, reasons for gains in international trade, long-term imbalances and exchange rates.

30. *Housing: Issues in Redevelopment* – Richard Dunnill and Eric Jackson (3, p. 6.1)
Investigates housing from the perspective of people's needs and wants, suppliers' differing viewpoints, and constraints on choice. Concepts covered include budgeting, goal conflicts, value judgements, resource allocation and social costs.

31. *An Income Distribution Simulation* – Kenneth J Neubeck (1, p. 264)
The teacher begins by giving the class a 10-question test. The correct answers are announced, and students are allocated up to 10 points for each question. The aggregate class score is computed, and students are then asked to decide in groups how to distribute this 'class income' earned through their work on the test. Possible solutions include equal shares, productivity, and guaranteed minimum income.

32. *The In Tray Exercise* (8)

Students are personnel managers of a factory employing 350 people. There are 12 memos in the tray, and participants have to decide which are the most important, what action is needed, and what will result.

33. *Jibon Ar Jumi* (14)

Simulates working life in a Bangladeshi village, and looks at the fundamental issues of land ownership. The exercise also considers the position of women, the introduction of new agricultural technology, and the trap of rural indebtedness.

34. *Juggernaut Ban* – Graham Teager (3, p. 17.1)

Students are given conflicting evidence about the ban on heavy lorries at certain times in London. Groups must use these data to convince others to support or oppose the continuation of this ban during a hypothetical review. Issues raised include the social costs of lorry movements and the implications of measures to redistribute such costs. Concepts include the distinction between private and social costs and opportunity costs.

35. *The Jute Game* (14)

Half the class represent Britain, half Bangladesh. Looks at jute production in both countries, and shows the effects on people's lives of decisions taken higher up, and the varying amount of power they have to alter their situation. Shows that wealth and poverty exist within as well as between countries.

36. *Keynesian Management of the Economy Game* – C J Brownless (7, 20. 1. 23)

First, students attempt to manage the economy using a single policy instrument – government expenditure. A further stage introduces incomes policy and devaluation options. Concepts covered include income–expenditure model, unemployment/inflation, surplus on balance of trade, deflation/reflation, J curve and devaluation.

37. *Labour Costs* – Sarah Veale (7, 24.4 121)

Produced by the TUC. Workers are told they have to accept lower wages or lose their jobs. It shows how unions make decisions. Students are members of a trade union in a public company, who receive a letter from the managing director, and call a union meeting to discuss their reaction to it.

38. *Land Use Planning in the Local Community* (16)

Based on a case study of a planning application for the change of use of a restaurant to a night club and restaurant in a predominantly residential area. Students are planning committee members. Introduces ideas of cost-benefit analysis.

39. *Leaving Home* – Pete Leech (3, p. 8.1)

Students are teenagers about to move into a place of their own with some friends. Individual role cards and accommodation cards provide a variety of situations for consideration. Concepts include opportunity costs, budgeting and demand and supply.

40. *Locating a Retail Outlet* – David Lines and Malcolm Surridge (3, p. 9.1)

This simulation is designed to investigate some of the factors which lie behind the decision to open a new branch of a large retail store. Concepts include location theory, opportunity costs, interpretation of data, the role of the economist, the accountant, the marketing and personnel managers.

41. *Location of Industry* – Brian Titley (3, p. 20.1)
Student groups are planners for a firm, and suggest possible locations for a micro-electronics company, a discount warehouse, a Japanese car manufacturer and an electricity generating station. Maps are provided which model general locational factors. Concepts include factors that affect industrial location, such as transport costs, bulk-reducing and increasing in production, footloose industries, economics of concentration, and the motives for government intervention and the various incentives it may offer.

42. *Managing the Economy* – Robert Paisley (3, p. 14.1)
Students are policy makers who are faced with high unemployment, inflation, etc. They may choose from a variety of policies, each of which has different effects on each target variable. Concepts covered include economic policy decisions and their effects, unemployment, inflation, PSBR, money supply, taxes, infrastructure, opportunity cost and economic models.

43. *Manomiya* (4 or 5)
Illustrates the role of women in African farming, and how development does not always benefit them. Includes board, colourful cards, instructions and background information for discussion.

44. *A Market for Roads* – Keith Wood (3, p. 22.1)
Students read a report of independent traffic consultants into road pricing in a small congested island (such as Hong Kong). They then role-play the Department of Transport, the AA, and local MPs, and each group proposes solutions to the problem. Concepts emerging include free market economic solutions, pricing, resource allocation, taxation and transport.

45. *Megatronics* – Chris Riley (11)
On the activities of a multinational company and its Welsh subsidiary, examining the latter's relationship with its parent company, the role of the government, and the importance of the firm to the local community. Highlights questions of redundancy, redeployment, government subsidiaries, possible takeover, creation of worker/management consortium. Concepts include social cost/benefit analysis.

46. *The Metal Box Business Game* (8)
Participants are lent £400,000 to set up in business marketing a product in competition with several other companies. Gives insight into the role of business manager, financing and operating a company and making decisions. This simulation is also available computerized, and an *Additional Dimension Component*, which includes 12 separate incidents, is available.

47. *Money, Output and Inflation* – David L McDougall (1, p. 90)
This simulation provides a simple illustration of the relationship between the money supply, output and the general price level. The class is divided into two groups, consumers and producers. The latter sell blocks of wood, and the consumers try to achieve as high a standard of living as possible, given their income constraint. The teacher, acting as government, adjusts the money supply each round.

48. *Monopolies and Mergers Commission* – Elizabeth Carrington (3, p. 5.1)
Students are divided into groups representing boards of directors and the MMC, and a public interest hearing is simulated, in which the proposed mergers are investigated. Concepts covered include the advantages of large-scale production, the trade-offs between profitability and employment, market share and monopoly control, and competition and costs of production.

49. *Muck in the Mock* – Nigel Wright, after Z S Starnawski (1, p. 248)
This is an environmental exercise, in which participants are consultant economists drawing up programmes to solve the problems of industrial waste deposits in the river Mock. Seven participants act as members of the river Mock Board, who receive submissions from the economics and attempt to agree on the solution to be adopted.

50. *Oligopoly Branding and Advertising Policy Game* – T E Widdows (7, 13. 4. 112)
Each class group represents a firm in an oligopolistic industry, seeking to enlarge its market share and increase profits. Each has to anticipate rivals' actions, and their possible effects. Illustrates interdependence in oligopoly, and the use of branding and advertising as non-price barriers to entry.

51. *An Oligopoly Game* – Myron Joseph and Rick Helm (1, p. 177)
Each student is a firm in a three-firm industry, and has to decide whether to charge a high, medium or low price for their product. Profits depend on the decision each firm makes in relation to its competitors. Collusion may be introduced. Illustrates the potential instability of an oligopolistic situation, and the possible benefits to firms in endeavouring to stabilize the market.

52. *Outerworld Trade* – Ken Jones (13)
The 5 planets of Outerworld each produce for internal consumption the same five major commodities, and they are about to start interplanetary trade. Concepts include production decisions, concepts in international trade, economic initiative and bargaining.

53. *The Paper Bag Game* (4)
Involves bag-making by players and discussion about life in a Calcutta bustee.

54. *The Paper Brick Game* – Ian Chambers (2, p. 51)
A simple production simulation, to demonstrate how production is organized, simple costing and pricing, marketing and collective bargaining.

55. *Paperchain: A Factory Production Line* – Elizabeth Carrington (3, p. 4.1)
Students simulate the production of paperchains in a factory production line. Covers the division of labour by process, negative aspects of production line work, and the firm as organizer of production.

56. *Penbrella: Problems of Expansion and Competition* – Ian Marcousé (3, p. 10.1)
Aims to set in a practical context the difficulties of expansion for a small firm. Students are producing the world's first umbrella that can fold up into the size of a pen. This is highly successful, and the firm experiences cash flow problems due to rapid expansion. Students have to try to maximize profits

over the next five years. It raises issues of raising finance, cash flow, marketing decisions, and competition.

57. *Pollards Premium Pork Pies* – Graham Teager (3, p. 18.1)
Students are members of the Pollard family, who have to study a financial statement and try to formulate a plan to rescue the firm. This involves calculation of costs, the discovery of more efficient uses of the firm's capital, pricing decisions, alternative sources of finance, and consensus decision-making. Concepts covered include costs, including fixed and variable, pricing, sources of finance and marketing.

58. *Population Crisis* – Andy Miller (3, p. 12.1)
Simulation in which participants are a committee deciding on policies for population planning. Members choose from 25 policy choices, ranking their most favoured, depending on cost constraints, likely popularity, whether free market or *dirigiste* methods are preferred by the government, etc.

59. *The Price is Right* – Simon Read (7, 25. 4. 176)
Manufacturing firms compete for orders on the basis of price. Covers the methods of pricing used by firms, including absorption and marginal cost pricing, and demand and supply for factors of production. This board game has students acting as companies aiming to maximize their profits.

60. *Pricing in a Perfectly Competitive Market* – Myron Joseph (1, p. 175)
Gives students the opportunity to participate in the determination of market price in a highly simplified market. Players are given buying or selling instructions in a wheat market, and mingle in the market place to obtain the best deal they can for their clients.

61. *Privatisation of Prisons* – Sarah Wilkinson (3, p. 21.1)
Simulates a meeting of a Select Committee of the House of Commons which has been established to investigate the prison system and to recommend changes. Students adopt the roles of members of different parties. Students have 24 policy statements which they discuss, and agree on policies to recommend. Concepts which arise include the nature of public goods, the profit motive, the interpretation and classification of information, privatization and costs of production.

62. *Production Record Sheets* (15)
Students are instructed to produce production record sheets, which are later used for recording the outcomes of the simulation. Demonstrates the implications of specialization, and the skills needed for successful cooperation in a team working towards agreed goals. Raises issues of requirements of cooperative activity, product quality and the working environment.

63. *Public Spending* (16)
Considers the opportunity costs of different patterns of government spending. Students decide on levels of taxation and expenditure as well as the mix of spending. Students represent political parties, and each group prepares a manifesto which is presented by the party secretary.

64. *The Real Aid Game* (5)
Participants have to judge a range of projects which might come forward for government aid. Illustrates issues affecting quality of aid.

65. *Redwards Engineering* – Alain Anderton (3, p. 1.1)
A collective bargaining role play, showing that there are strong pressures for different parties in a dispute to come to a negotiated settlement. Also illustrates the possibility that different unions might have different perspectives on the same issue.

66. *A Regional Policy Role-Play* – Des Monk (7, 22. 1. 14)
A motor-bike company is about to set up a new plant, either in S. Wales, Liverpool or London. Students acting various roles have to decide where to locate the plant, using the concepts of availability of raw materials, proximity to the market and transport facilities.

67. *Regional Policy and Regional Planning: Aluminium Smelter* – D Golby and S J Hurd (12)
Students follow the procedures associated with a major development proposal: the public enquiry, representations made by major interest groups, and the outcome. The material relates to the closure of the aluminium smelter at Invergordon.

68. *Rock Island* – Ken Jones (13)
Rock Island is a poor country with a primitive transport system, but it discovered off-shore oil a decade ago. The government has used the oil revenues to build motorways, new towns and holiday centres, etc. A questionnaire asks people for their preferences, prior to an election. Topics covered include the economics of sudden wealth, the problems of road transport, and private and social costs and benefits.

69. *Ruraplan* (8)
Concerns the economic development of a community, introducing problems associated with business awareness and community life. Background material provides information about the location, while specialist briefs describe the tasks which the participants will be given, and the problems they are likely to face.

70. *St Philip* (4)
Concerns issues surrounding tourist development on a Third World Island, to help students understand arguments for and against development of large scale tourism in the Third World.

71. *Selling the Flag* – Ken Jones (13)
The mid-Atlantic country of Atlan has no government. An election has returned four parties in equal numbers. There will be a special parliamentary debate on the main election issue – the sale of Atlan. Concepts include the economic and political aspects of any government privatizing its service, industries or utilities.

72. *Stance* (9)
A major set of simulations based on the detergent industry. Groups form companies which have to make a series of decisions on 10 set issues, to determine the best possible outcome for their firm, its employees and shareholders. Roles include production, personnel, engineering and planning managers, supervisor and trade union representative. The 10 issues cover requirements for increased capacity, quality, consultation, staffing/work patterns, health

and safety, new technology, discipline, maintenance arrangements, packing materials and human relations.

73. *The Standard of Living Game* – Paul Coates (10)

Six families are shipwrecked on an island without resources, and start by producing for self-sufficiency, then begin to specialize, in order to maximize their standard of living.

74. *Starpower* – Gary Shirts (4)

Trading game exploring power relationships. Players are given trading tokens, which are distributed unequally. After several trading rounds, rule changes strengthen the hand of the high achievers.

75. *Survival* – Bill Jennings (1, p. 142)

This simulation is suitable to use as an introduction to the concepts of economic resources, basic economic questions, different economic systems, economic interdependence and specialization. The class is lost on an Arctic island, with little hope of rescue. Their object is survival, and they need to satisfy their basic needs for food, shelter and clothing – but they can only use the equipment supplied.

76. *Survival on the Island of Ikeda* – Elizabeth Carrington (3, p. 3.1)

Students are set the task of surviving on a desert island, first as individuals, then as groups. Concepts include division of labour/specialization, consumption/investment, and factors of production.

77. *Takeover* – Julian Stanley (3, p. 16.1)

This exercise simulates take-overs in the brewing industry. Each student group directs a brewery, and aims to increase turnover to avoid being taken over. The class may also explore other criteria for success, such as rate of growth, size of cash reserves, size of debt, and profits as a percentage of turnover.

78. *Taxation and Spending: Who Pays?* – Richard Thorne (3, p. 19.1)

Each student is a major political figure. The party, in preparation for the next general election, has made a commitment to increased expenditure. The revenue is to be raised from taxation, but no decision has yet been made on precisely which taxes are to be raised. Each group has to put forward proposals and justify them to the rest of the class. They must also justify their expenditure proposals. Concepts include the major forms of taxation and government expenditure, and the opportunity costs of public decision-making.

79. *A Trade Game* (4)

Players are consumers, traders and retailers of commodities such as bananas, sugar or coffee. Descriptive paper available free, and the game can readily be prepared by the teacher.

80. *The Trading Game* (4 or 5)

Aim is to help players understand more clearly how trade can affect the prosperity of a country. Clear, illustrated instructions for organizing game; also points for leaders and guidelines for discussion.

81. *Tunic Trade* – Richard Dunnill (2, p. 6)

Pencils, rulers and scissors game to demonstrate concepts of subsistence and surplus, and to introduce concepts of scarcity, resources, specialization and division of labour. Groups are firms producing cotton tunics.

82. *Wages* (15)
Uses news-cuttings and a wage negotiation to introduce the institutional framework of industrial relations and the processes involved in pay bargaining. Highlights the importance of value positions.

83. *The Widget Game* – K Light (1, p. 73)
This production simulation involves students making widgets from paper and paper clips, to illustrate four sources of efficiency in the production process: specialization, education, motivation and scale of enterprise.

84. *World Control* (6)
A game of world trade options, for age 10 upwards, for 3–7 people. Board game in which players are industrialized, developing or newly industrialized countries. World monopolies and multi-national companies are created. Aims to show how present world economic system works, how a new international economic order could function, and what happens with greater investment in human resources.

85. *The World Feast Game* (4)
Game to help players understand issues concerning the production, distribution and consumption of world food.

Index of concepts

Sources of simulations

1. Whitehead, D J (ed) (1979) *Handbook for Economics Teachers.* Heinemann Educational, London.
2. Whitehead, D J (ed) (1980) *Economics Education. A Second Handbook for Economics Teachers.* Heinemann Educational, London.
3. Whitehead, D J (ed) (1988) *Trade-offs: Simulations and Role Plays for Economics.* Longman, Harlow.
4. Centre for World Development Education, Regent's College, Inner Circle, Regent's Park, London NW1 4NS.
5. Oxfam, 274, Banbury Rd, Oxford, OX2 7DX.
6. Tanzania Import, PO Box 165, S-581 02 Linköping, Sweden.
7. *Economics*, the journal of The Economics Association, 1A Keymer Road, Hassocks, West Sussex BN6 8AD. Key: 24. 4. 121 means volume 24, part 4, page 121.
8. Hobsons Press, Bateman St, Cambridge, CB2 1LZ.
9. Unilever Educational Liaison, PO Box 68, Unilever House, London EC4P 4BQ.
10. Coates, P (1989) *Business Venture.* OUP, Milton Keynes. Oxford, p. 11.
11. Longman Group UK Ltd, Longman House, Burnt Mill, Harlow, Essex CM20 2JE.
12. Available from SJ Hurd, Staffs Polytechnic, Stoke-on-Trent ST4 2DF.
13. Jones, K (1989) *A Sourcebook of Management Simulations.* Kogan Page, London.
14. *Dhaka to Dundee.* Leeds Development Education Centre, 151–3 Cardigan Rd., Leeds LS6 1LJ.
15. 'Young person as producer' (1985), in *Understanding Economics.* Longman, Harlow.
16. 'Young person as citizen', (1985) in *Understanding Economics.* Longman, Harlow.
17. Anderton, AG (1986) *Economics for GCSE.* Collins, London.
18. Banking Information Service, 10, Lombard St, London EC3V 9AT.

16 A Level and GCSE Business Studies Resources

David Lines

The value of all teaching aids is highly subjective, and will depend on a number of variables such as the size of the class, the physical environment, and the characteristics of the pupils. The teacher's knowledge and skills are also vital ingredients but choice is always limited by the amount of money which is available.

Even if the cash constraint did not exist, A level Business Studies suffered in the past from a lack of good resources because its fairly recent entry into the Sixth Form curriculum resulted in a relatively small and therefore unattractive market to publishers. There were in fact a few specific books offered, and there was material to be found written for BTEC, but all of it possessed major flaws which could be readily identified and which became a constant irritation.

Support was, and still is provided for teachers of the subject by the Cambridge Business Studies Trust[1] which sells a teaching file covering the main topics of all the currently offered syllabuses. In addition, the Trust provides visits and caters for other INSET needs, including a week-long residential course held in June every year.[2]

The Examination Boards provide resources lists, and since they are usually written to fit into the specific and somewhat different requirements of each examination, they can be used as a prime source. Some of these lists are, however, badly in need of updating, and should be treated with caution where this is evident.

Teaching resources can be conveniently divided up into several categories:

- Text books
- Simulations and role plays
- Computer software
- Magazines

Comments made on each of the resources mentioned will necessarily be subjective, but they represent the views of a number of highly experienced practising teachers throughout the country. I am particularly grateful to one of my M.A. students, Mrs Jan Burnett for her contributions to this research.

Text books

The following list contains what may be termed the subject's 'best sellers'. This does not mean, of course, that they are necessarily the best books; it may be more a reflection of the relative lack of competition referred to above. It is therefore advisable to obtain inspection copies before any decision to purchase is made.

An Integrated Approach to Business Studies by Jewell, BR, Pitman, 1990. ISBN 0-273-03249-6.

Specifically written for A Level. Initial reactions have been highly complimentary. Readers have admired the clear lay-out and the use of case study, stimulus and data-response materials.

Business Studies by Hammond, S, Longman, 1991. ISBN 0-582-05705-1.

Mrs Hammond was Chief Examiner for the AEB until 1985, and this book reflects her experience and knowledge of the subject. The first edition (1988) was almost the first attempt to provide comprehensive coverage of all the main syllabusus in one book, and as a result was somewhat limited in certain areas. It proved to be an extremely popular book despite this, and the second edition has gone some way to counter the criticisms. A Teacher's Guide should be available in 1991. The second edition has been written to complement *Business Case Studies* by Marcousé, I and Lines, D. In addition satellite texts, edited by Mrs Hammond, are due for publication in 1991.

Business Studies – An Integrated Approach by Fearns, P Hodder and Stoughton, 1989. ISBN 0-340-41462-6.

The author was the first Chief Examiner for the AEB, and this book has appeared on their booklist from its inception. For these reasons Fearns still has a strong following, and has gone to several editions, but in many eyes it remains a somewhat superficial approach.

Understanding Business Series edited by Barker, R, Longman.

There are a number of books in this series which were specifically written for the Cambridge Advanced level examination. Most of the authors have been, or are, Chief Examiners for the Cambridge Examination Board. Each one of the books is highly detailed, but some overlap, while others have only a passing relevance to syllabuses other than Cambridge's. They are also now rather out of date, although by 1991 they will have all been revised and condensed to only four books, plus one on case studies.

Decision Making in Organisations by Clifford, J, 1976. ISBN 0-582-35539-7.

This is regarded as the 'core book' in the series. It uses some interesting case studies, and still provides a valuable overview. It is now very outdated and rather old fashioned.

Accounting and Decision Making by Corbett, P, 1982. ISBN 0-582-35104-9.

It falls into the book-keeping trap in places, and there is certainly a great deal of detail which is not necessary for many syllabuses. There is also a severe overlap with the Finance book in the same series.

Economy and Decision Making by Donaldson, P and Clifford, J, 1980. ISBN X-19-16959-4.

In many ways a difficult book, not so much in content, but more in its context, because there is a tendency to emphasize economic concepts rather than their constraints on business.

Financial Decisions by Middleton, D, 1983. ISBN 0-582-35401-3.

There is some excellent material in this book, but the overlap with the Accounting book is too great.

Marketing Decisions by Tinniswood, P, 1981, ISBN 0-582-35543-5.

An entertaining book for a stimulating part of the syllabus. The examples now clearly need updating.

People and Decisions by Worrall, N, 1980. ISBN 0-582-35540-09.2.

A rather hazy book, but one containing some interesting exercises and simulations.

Production Decisions by Powell, J, 1978. ISBN 0-582-35544-3.

A lively and well written book, but one which is applicable to only a few syllabuses.

Business Case Studies by Marcousé, I and Lines, D, Longman, 1990 ISBN 0-582-05779-9.

Containing 79 case studies of different lengths and degrees of difficulty, this book, or one similar to it has been needed for some considerable time. There are also sections on examination techniques using case studies. The book is designed to complement Hammond (*op. cit.*)

Business Studies by Needham, D and Dransfield, R, McGraw Hill, 1990. ISBN 0-07-707224-3.

This is the first genuine attempt to be comprehensive in the way that text books are for other subject areas. The general response has been highly favourable towards this new entrant to the market.

Business Organisations and their Environments by Glew, M, Watts, I and Wells, S, Heinemann, 1987. ISBN 0-453-45906-6.

Although written more directly for BTEC, the two volumes under the same name contain much of relevance to A level Business Studies.

Business Studies – An Introduction by Dyer, D and Chambers, I, Longman, 1987. ISBN 0-582-35603-2.

This was the first book written specifically for GCSE, and has proved very popular in that market. It is regarded as being more applicable to the more able student at that level, and so makes an excellent introductory text at A level for those students meeting the subject for the first time. Other books are perhaps less well known, but all have their supporters.

They have been grouped together in terms of syllabus area, although of course many of them overlap into more than one.

(a) The organization in its context

Discover Business and Industrial Society by Teager, G and Butlin, D, Pitman, 1988. ISBN 0-273-02848-0.

Exploring Industry and Enterprise by Dransfield, R and Needham, D, Cassell, 1989. ISBN 0-304-31575-3.

The Firm and its Environment by Barback R H, Philip Allen, 1984. ISBN 0-86003-628-3.

Finding About Series, by Allen, S (ed.). Six books in the series. Hobsons Publications for CRAC 1983-87.

'Guide to . . .' Series, The Banking Information Service. These resources are free on request.

In Perspective. This is a series covering a number of areas, CRAC.

Organisations at Work by Frampton, M, Pitman, 1988. ISBN 0-273-02646-1.

Starting Up by Jones, G, Pitman, 1988. ISBN 0-273-02896-0.

The Organisation in its Environment by Beardshaw, J and Palfreyman, J, Pitman, 1990. ISBN 0-273-03268-2.

The Organisation in its Environment by Hawkins and Jones, Oxford University Press, 1988. ISBN 0-19-833535-0.

Understanding Industry by Hogarth, A, Edward Arnold, 1983 ISBN 0-7131-0813-4.

Understanding Industry booklets. Published by Understanding Industry.

Understanding Industry Now by Stefanou, R, Heinemann, 1989. ISBN 0-435-45110-3.

Understanding Organisations by Handy C, Penguin, 3rd. edn, 1986. ISBN 0-14-009110-6.

The World of Business by Smidman, M, Heinemann, 1989. ISBN 0-435-45552-4.

(b) Accounting and finance

Accounting 2 by Wood, F and Townsley, J, Pitman, 1989. ISBN 0-273-02974-6.

Finance by Hopkins, J, Pitman, 1988. ISBN 0-273-02877-4.

Financial Accounting by Blake, J, Hutchinson, 1988. ISBN 0-09-161641-7.

Financial Management for the Small Business by Barrow, C, Kogan Page, 1988. ISBN 0-85091-566-0.

How to Understand and Use Company Accounts by Warren, R, Business Books, 1990. ISBN 0-09-174605-1.

Mastering Principles of Accounts by Scott, R, Macmillan, 1982. ISBN 0-333-30446-2.

Management Accounting for Non-Financial Managers by Bell, M, Bradshaw, D and Hermann, M, Longman, 1987. ISBN 0-582-35527-3.

Techniques for Accounting by Bradshaw, D, Hermann, M and Bell, M, Longman, 1987. ISBN 0-582-35527-3.

Understanding Company Accounts by Bird, P and Rutherford, B, Pitman, 1989. ISBN 0-273-02889-8.

Understanding Company Accounts by Rothenberg, B and Newman, J, Kogan Page, 1988. ISBN 0-86367-191-8.

(c) The economic environment

Approaching Economics by Perry, A, Stanley Thornes, 1990. ISBN 0-7487-0370-5.

Labour Markets & Management Economics by Shafto, T, & Mallier, T, Hutchinson, 1989. ISBN 0-09-173166-6

Organisation and Administration for Business by Whitehead, D, Hutchinson, 1989. ISBN 0-09-175656-1.

The UK Economy: A Manual of Applied Economics by Prest AR, Weidenfeld & Nicolson, 1989. ISBN 0-279-79691-7.

(d) The legal environment

Business Law by Marsh, SB and Soulsby JR, McGraw Hill, 1989. ISBN 0-07-707253-7.

Company Law by Thomas, C, Hodder & Stoughton, 1985. ISBN 0-340-38479-4.

(e) Marketing

Advertising by Jefkins, FW, M & E Handbooks, 1985. ISBN 0-7121-0664-2.

Basic Marketing – Principles and Practice by Cannon, T, Cassell, ISBN 0-304-31411-0.

Marketing by Maxwell, R, Macmillan Education, 1989. ISBN 0-334-48790-7.

Elements of Marketing by Morden, AR, D.P. Publications, 1987. ISBN 0-905-43588-5.

Marketing in Practice by Leader, WG and Kyritsis N, Stanley Thornes, 1990. ISBN 0-7487-0512-0.

Marketing by Giles, GB, M & E Handbooks, 1990. ISBN 0-7121-1420-3.

Marketing by Stapleton, J, Hodder & Stoughton, 1984. ISBN 0-340-33920-9.

Marketing by Martin, E, Mitchell Beazley, 1983. ISBN 0-85533-442-8.

Marketing & Product Development by Littler, P, Philip Allen, 1984. ISBN 0-86003-633-2

(f) People in business

Employment Relations in Industrial Society by Goodman, JC, Philip Allen, 1984. ISBN 0-86003-635-9.

Managing Industrial Conflict by Meredeen, S, Hutchinson, 1988. ISBN 0-09-173226-3.

People, Communication & Organisation by Evans, DW, Pitman, 1990. ISBN 0-273-02588-0.

People in Organisations by Harrison, J and Bell, V, Pitman, 1987. ISBN 0-273-02283-0.

People in Organisations by Robinson, D, Page, S and Fella, B, Stanley Thornes, 1988. ISBN 0-7487-0326-8.

Success in Management: Personnel by Hackett, P, John Murray, 1985. ISBN 0-7195-4713-X.

Understanding Industrial Relations by Farnham, D and Pimlott, J, Cassell, 1990. ISBN 0-304-31794-2.

A Textbook of Human Resource Management by Thomason, G, IPM, 1988. ISBN 0-85292-403-8.

(g) Quantitative methods

Facts from Figures by Moroney, MJ, Penguin, 1990. ISBN 0-14-013540-5.

How to Lie with Statistics by Huff, D, Penguin, 1973. ISBN 0-14-021300-7.

Statistics for Business Studies by Gregory, D and Ward, H, McGraw Hill, 1987. ISBN 0-07-084606-5.

Statistics Without Tears by Rowntree, D, Penguin, 1981. ISBN 0-14-022326-6.

(h) General reference books

Some of these books are very large and quite expensive. They are the sort of which one might buy a single copy for library use.

A Dictionary of Economics and Business by Stiegler and Thomas (eds), Pan, 1986. ISBN 0-330-28819-9.

Business Decisions by Chilver, J, Macmillan, 1983. ISBN 0-333-34498-7.

Management: Theory and Practice by Cole, GA, D.P. Publications, 1990. ISBN 1-870941-60-8.

Mastering Basic Management by Eyre, EC, Macmillan, 1985. ISBN 0-33-37309-X.

Strategic Management by David, FR, Merrill, 1989. ISBN 0-675-20938-2.

(i) Teachers' reference books

Business Education: A Handbook for Schools, TVEI, 1990.

Directory of Business Studies Resources by Jones, K and Taylor, D. (eds) Pitman, 1989. ISBN 0-273-030922.

Teaching Business Education by Cullimore, D (ed.), Business Education Publishers Limited, 1990. ISBN 0-907679-34-X.

Simulations and role plays

(See also Chapter 15)
Briefcase, by Werner, J (ed.) Understanding Industry 1986, ISBN 1-870051-00-9.

Business Case Studies by Hobsons for CRAC. ISBN 0-86021-951-8.

BTEC National: An implementation Strategy. Case Studies and Assignments in Business by Kelsey, B, Parker, M Rogers, and G, Pitman, 1989. ISBN 0-273-03034-5.

Communications Skills - 130 Assignments CRAC, ISBN 0-86021-942-9.

The In-Tray Exercise, Hobsons for CRAC. ISBN 0-86021-657-8.

The Enterprise Game (Board Game) sponsored by Lloyds Bank and BP.

The Enterprise Pack by Jamieson, A, CRAC, ISBN 1-85324-216-0.

Megatronics - Focus on a Firm by Riley, C, Longman, ISBN 0-582-22522-1.

The Mini Co. Kit by Bray, E, Longman, ISBN 0-582-38858-9.

Project Business Plan (including Video) by Straw, J, Longman, ISBN 0-582-17424-4.

Ruraplan by Hobsons for CRAC, 1988. ISBN 1-85324-082-6.

Trade-offs: Simulations and Role Plays for Economics by Whitehead, D, (ed.), Longman, 1988. ISBN 0-582-00333-4.

The Trading Business - Case Studies in Exporting by ECATT on behalf of the DTI, Longman. ISBN 0-582-00614-7.

Computer software

(See also Chapter 17)

Accounts Trainer by Riddler, G and Barker, B, Pitmansoft, ISBN 0-273-02367-7. Suitable for IBM PC Machines.

Airfares, Pitmansoft, ISBN 0-273-02899-5. Suitable for BBC and Nimbus Machines.

Balance Sheet Analysis by Riddle, G and Barker, B, Pitmansoft. ISBN 0-273-02868-5. Suitable for IBM PC Machines.

Beat the Boss, BBRC software. Suitable for BBC and Nimbus Machines.

BIS-ness: 4 Case Studies on Enterprise, BIS. Suitable for BBC/48OZ machines.

Break Even Analysis, Profit Planning and Analysis, BBRC software. Suitable for BBC and Nimbus Machines.

The Business Plan, Pitmansoft. ISBN 0-273-02695-X. Suitable for BBC and Nimbus Machines.

Business Documents, Pitmansoft. ISBN 0-273-02705-0. Suitable for BBC and Nimbus Machines.

Buy 'em Down, BBRC software. Suitable for BBC and Nimbus Machines.

The Castaway Shirt Company, BBRC software. Suitable for BBC and Nimbus Machines.

Cost Benefit Analysis, Longman. Suitable for BBC, Nimbus and ARC machines.

The Cement Business Game, BBRC software. Suitable for BBC and Nimbus Machines.

Crisis Management, BBRC software. Suitable for BBC and Nimbus Machines.

Dealer by Atherton, D, Pitmansoft. Suitable for Nimbus.

Diary Planner, Pitmansoft. ISBN 0-273-02218-0. Suitable for BBC Machines.

Don't Panic, BBRC software. Suitable for BBC and Nimbus Machines.

Electronic Mail, Pitmansoft. ISBN 0-273-02221-0. Suitable for BBC Machines.

Estate Agent, Longman. Suitable for BBC machines.

Exchequer by Atherton, D, Pitmansoft. Suitable for Nimbus Machines.

Finstat – financial statistics database, BIS. Suitable for BBB/480Z machines.

Five Simple Business Games, Hobsons. ISBN 0-86021-765-5. Suitable for BBC Machines.

Handling Time, BBRC software. Suitable for BBC and Nimbus Machines.

Hotel, Pitmansoft. ISBN 0-273-02219-9. Suitable for BBC Machines.

Hyperbook, Longman. Suitable for Nimbus, BBC and IBM PC Machines.

Intervention, Longman. Suitable for BBC machines.

It's Your Future (with spreadsheet tutorial), BIS. Suitable for BBB and 480Z machines.

Mini Office (an integrated package), General Spreadsheet Software. Suitable for BBC Machines.

Metal Box Game, CRAC. ISBN 0-86021-646-2 (basic game) and 1-85324-188-1 (additional dimension). Suitable for 480Z Machines.

Money Problems, BIS. Suitable for BBC and 480Z machines.

Payslip, Pitmansoft. ISBN 0-273-02160-5. Suitable for BBC and Nimbus Machines.

Sixgam by Randall, K and Greenwood, A, Pitmansoft. ISBN 0-273-02088-9. Suitable for BBC and Nimbus Machines.

Stalebread, Tutor Software. Suitable for BBC and Nimbus Machines.

Stock Control, Pitmansoft. ISBN 0-273-02683-6. Suitable for BBC Machines.

Stratlife, Longman. Suitable for BBC, Nimbus and IBM PC Machines.

Sucker – A Business Game, Longman. Suitable for BBC and Nimbus Machines.

Teddytronic – The Story of a Firm, Longman. *Suitable for BBC, Nimbus and Apple Machines.*

Trading Firms, BIS. Suitable for BBC and 480Z machines.

Understanding Business Studies and Commerce by Whitcomb, A and Beckwith, P, Pitmansoft. ISBN 0-273-02938-X/02939-8. Suitable for BBC and Nimbus Machines.

Understanding Economics, Longman. Suitable for BBC, 480Z, 380Z, Nimbus and Apple machines.

Trading Firms (Exchange Rates), Bank Information Service.

Unisim Business Game, Unilever. Suitable for BBC and IBM PC Machines.

UK Economy: An Introductory Database by Beharrell, A, Pitmansoft. ISBN 0-273-02638-0. Suitable for BBC Machines.

Workers & Machines Longman. Suitable for BBC, Nimbus and ARC machines.

Videos

Recent arrangements with the Broadcasting authorities have helped the legal position with regard to copying material shown on television. As a result, the major television channels are making efforts to ease the finding of programmes appropriate to specific subject areas.

Many local authorities have a centralized copying arrangement, which teachers should confirm individually. Like any other teaching resource, the way in which videos are used will depend on the teacher and his/her requirements.

The Bank Information Service, for instance, produces a series of free films which may be appropriate. Others will be found in their catalogue:

Banking Business, The
Banking on Industry
Credit Casualty
Golden Rules
History of Money
It Doesn't Grow on Trees
Putting You in the Picture
Simple Account, A

Likewise the Stock Exchange offers free hire on *Spectrum – Stock Exchange Information for Teachers*, and 3i offer *Management Buy-Outs*.

Audio tapes

How to Pass Advanced Level Business Studies by Lines, D, Anforme Publications Ltd, 1991.

GCSE Business Studies textbooks

Butler, D, 1989, *Business Studies*, Oxford University Press.
Dyer, D and Chambers, I, 1987, *Business Studies. An Introduction*, Longman.
Hammond, S, 1991, *Active Business Studies*, Longman.
Huggett, R, 1988, *Business Studies for GCSE*, Collins.
Ison, S and Pye, K, 1988, *GCSE Business Studies*, Longman.
Parsons, C and Cain, J, 1989, *Investigating Business*, Longman.
Smidman, M, 1989, *The World of Business*, Heinemann Educational.
Tayfoor, V, 1989, *Examining Business Studies*, Nelson.

Other GCSE Business Studies books

Barrett, R, 1991, *Business Studies Skills*, Stanley Thornes.
Dransfield, R, 1989, *Business Studies Investigations*, Shell Education Service.
Dransfield, R and Needham, D, 1989, *Exploring Industry and Enterprise*, Cassell.
Huggett, R, 1989, *Assignments in Business Education*, John Murray.
Huggett, R, 1991, *Business Case Studies*, Cambridge University Press.
Ison, S and Lines, D, 1989, *GCSE Business Studies Coursework*, Longman.
Smith, J, 1990, *Modular Business Studies*, Longman.
Stefanou, R, *Understanding Industry Now*, Heinemann Educational. Also Teachers' Guide available from Understanding Industry.

Wallace, D, 1991, *Business Studies and Commerce Coursework Pack*, Causeway Press.
Wallace, D, 1991, *Coursework in Business Studies and Commerce – A Student Guide*, Causeway Press.

Notes

1. The Cambridge Business Studies Trust has its office at 22 Nene Crescent, Oakham, Leicestershire. It provides many resources, including expertise in the form of the Director and the Assistant Director of the Trust who travel the country offering help and advice to schools and colleges for the price of their travelling expenses.
2. Details of INSET courses can be obtained from the Trust's office at Oakham.

17 Economics and Business Education Software

David Whitehead

This chapter attempts to narrow down the choice of computer software, so that teachers and lecturers with small budgets can start their collection with only the most outstanding programs. But is it worth bothering with computer assisted learning (CAL) at all? According to Professor Lumsden, the doyen of CAL, it has a comparative advantage in only two areas: simulations and data handling. Nevertheless, many packages simply replace conventional teaching with programmed learning of concepts or batteries of multiple choice questions. Some actually put the textbook on to the screen.

Professor Walstad, a leading American Economics educator, maintains that CAL has been oversold, and we are already seeing the same sort of reaction against this 'nine days' wonder' as occurred with educational TV in the 1970s, CAL is unlikely ever to supplant the teacher, but as with most teaching techniques, moderate use is probably justified, if only to provide some variety and enhance motivation.

The market for programs is rather weak, as publishers will endorse. With such a limited market, sales are rarely sufficient to obtain a reasonable return on the publisher's investment. The only reason that so much software is available is that many developers' time has not been paid for at market rates.

Ignorance about what programs are available is surprisingly widespread. Even some teachers who *use* CAL have not heard of *Running the British Economy*, undoubtedly the program with the highest profile in the UK.

Dealing first with programs involving simulations or games suitable for A Level or above, these may be divided into two categories: macroeconomic decision-making and business games. Of the former, *Running the British Economy (RBE)* (Longman) is by far the most frequently used. Large numbers of students take part annually in a national competition, with regional heats and a grand final in Edinburgh. While the program is rather costly, the model will now remain unchanged for four years. *RBE* requires students to run the economy for ten years, deciding annually on government expenditure, tax rates and the money supply. The simulation has a 'practice' and a 'real' version, the latter incorporating exogenous shocks which disrupt players' strategies. The government has a welfare function, and the object is to maximize the welfare points gained over the ten years. The 1990 version has many new features, which mirror the preoccupations of economic policy-makers: supply-side effects; the problem of uncontrollable imports; the importance of capital flows; and the exchange rate. This version also includes alternative welfare functions (which spikes the criticism that the devisers are imposing their own values on users). Presentation is also much more sophisti-cated, with improved colour, graphics, statistical record-keeping and flexible practice run capabilities. The supporting booklet contains full briefing notes, including a fictional account of a student team's run, with dialogue between them and their professor on the likely impact of their policies.

As a motivating activity, *RBE* is without parallel. But it is often difficult to get students to think through carefully the likely consequences of their deci-sions, rather than just plumping for a policy and hoping for the best. The model is quite complex, as the authors drolly comment: 'this appears compli-cated for a good reason – it is complicated.'

Another cognate simulation worth buying is *Chancellor* (McGraw Hill). This program casts the user or teams in the role of Chancellor of the Exchequer, and shows how decisions to control the economy are affected by trade-offs and uncertainties. It gives a synoptic view of modern macroeconomics, from the Keynesian monetarist and neo-classical perspectives. Players have to manage an economy over an 8-year period, by manipulating five controls.

Plenty of business games are to be recommended at this level. Recent publi-cations include *Crisis Management* (RBRC Software) and *The Cement Business Game* (RBRC Software). The former involves decision-making in a company manufacturing disposable shirts. The latter gives insights into constraints on business decision-making, for example because electricity costs vary at different times of day, and legal controls exist on the distribution of goods by road. Another simulation from the same supplier, *Beat the Boss* (RCBC Software), is the vehicle for a national 'Young Business People of the Year' competition. *The Paraffin File* (BP) concentrates on the 'marketing mix', with reference to price, advertising, and sales staff, in an oligopolistic market. *Sixgam* (Pitmansoft) has teams acting as firms selling word processors in inter-national markets. Its aim is to test players' understanding of such concepts as fixed and variable costs, demand curves, and cost-based pricing. *Airfares* (Pitmansoft) is a business game, in which competing teams of transatlantic airline operators decide on services, fares, meals, the number of planes and the advertising budget over a period of one to eight quarters.

Several simulations have been devised specifically for 14–16-year-olds. For example, *Stock Market* (Longman) requires users to become economic ana-lysts, and predict how six companies' share prices might change as a result of certain news items. Each team is given a notional £100, and has to decide what, if any, shares to buy. The game is competitive: the team which makes the best predictions also makes the highest capital gain. In *Sucker* (Longman) students make managerial decisions about the operation of a company mak-ing vacuum cleaners. *The Filling Station* (BP) is a computerized version of a pencil and paper simulation devised more than 20 years ago by Chris Jelley.

Five garages have to decide on the price they will charge for petrol, and whether they will use promotions to increase sales, over a period of 12 months of decision rounds. Performance is measured by market share, profit and a management efficiency rating.

Another 'best buy' for GCSE Economics or Business Studies is *Trading Firms* (BIS). This four-program suite begins with a simulation of the impact of exchange rate changes on the purchase of raw materials. The second program concerns the purchase of foreign currency on spot or forward exchange markets. Next, students have to set a price for profit maximization in an overseas market after changes in the exchange rate. Finally, a team game based on a UK knitwear company brings together various elements from the other simulations.

Workers and Machines (Longman) is a substantial program, simulating production decisions for a firm manufacturing supermarket trolleys. Students have to allocate workers between three tasks in the production process: cutting, shaping and welding. In *Balance of Payments* (Longman) students take on the role of the Chancellor of the Exchequer, in order to respond to the Prime Minister's request to establish equilibrium in the current balance. *Teddytronic* (Longman) is a team game in which students manage a firm making electronic teddy bears. Decisions must be made on output, workforce and wages, prices, advertising and loans. Once teams have mastered the variables, the exercise is highly motivating and can transform classes' attitude to the subject. Finally in this section, *Alarmco* (Software Productions), while originally devised for a mathematics project, is a business simulation in which firms manufacture and market burglar alarms. They have to hire a workshop, spend on wages and advertising, take out an overdraft and try to maximize profits.

For databases, *Macroeconomic Trends* (Longman) enables students to examine time series data on the UK economy for the past three decades. Particularly useful is the facility to examine two time series simultaneously, with or without a time lag. The data may be converted to indices and percentage changes, displayed in line and scatter graphs, and lines of best fit and correlation coefficients may be obtained.

Similarly up-to-date is *Comparative Economic Data* (Longman), which permits comparison of statistics from *Regional Trends* with similar information from *World Development Report* (from 15 countries). The regional data comprise 19 items, and apart from obvious ones like population and net migration, include for example school leaver examination results, average household income, the percentage of households with certain durable goods (students will be fascinated by the regional variations in ownership of washing machines, fridges, TVs and phones), and smoke and sulphur dioxide pollution. The 15 countries include, *inter alia*, Ethiopia, Nigeria, Malaysia, UK, USA, Brazil, West Germany and Japan. The data set comprises 31 indices, many of which permit comparisons with the British regional statistics. Another valuable database is *Finstat* (BIS), which comprises 58 financial statistics for use by A level students.

One of the problems of the first generation of databases for microcomputers was that it was often quicker to look up statistics in a book than retrieve them from the database. Another was the difficulty of manipulating the data and performing statistical analyses upon it. The following two programs seek to rectify these faults.

SECOS (Statistics for Education) is designed to be easy and fast to use, and to include all the main data analysis functions. It is a simple procedure for teachers or students to create their own data sets, for example on local or regional trends. One group could be responsible for a price survey, another for housing, etc. Data are stored in tables which are accessible via a simple tree structure. All the tables may be modified, and calculations performed on lines, columns or whole tables. The package does not aim to be comprehensive, but it includes these frequently required functions: sort, time-lag, indices, growth rate, proportions, (moving) averages, correlation, standard deviation and line of best fit. The program is accompanied by a 112-page manual which provides an introductory tour using a step-by-step sample exercise to illustrate the main functions, a reference section, and a guide for teachers with tips on class-room organization.

EURECO (Statistics for Education) runs under *SECOS*. The statistics (from Eurostat), are on population, employment, national accounts, principal aggre-gates, money and finance, foreign trade by zone and product, balance of pay-ments, energy, and public finance. Not only are all 12 EC countries included, but the same data are given for the USA and Japan, which is useful for compar-ative investigations. An 88-page manual includes extensive teacher/student exercises. It is planned to update the package annually. If teachers wish to use the program didactically, they may spice their exposition with examples from all over the EC. Alternatively, they may choose to select some of the eight investi-gations supplied in the manual. Hypotheses include, for example, 'When popu-lation growth slows down the proportion of elderly dependents tends to increase, and the proportion of young people declines'. The level of treatment assumes that a formal economics course, such as A level, is being taken. These exercises provide rich opportunities for practical coursework, in which students may apply their analytical skills and learn about the economies of other Euro-pean countries. Moreover, as Hurd comments: 'Using data which has [sic] not been pre-selected or modified to show desired relationships, as is often the case with published data response exercises, can have a liberating and energising effect on students, which actually strengthens their commitment to the sub-ject.' (Hurd, 1990, p. 19).

A third category of program seeks to teach large swathes of theory or indi-vidual concepts. Some of these CAL packages are overambitious (and overpriced!). A recommended purchase is *Basic Principles of Microeconomics: Demand, Supply and Competition* (AVP). These eight programs, pitched at A level standard, help students to reinforce their understanding of neo-classical microeconomics. Despite the programmed learning style of presentation, students have to be active in responding to the program's directions. Another worthwhile buy is *Growth under Fixed Exchange Rates* (Longman), which sets a 1960s scenarios of fixed exchange rates, and asks students to achieve a steady rate of growth plus equilibrium in the balance of payments, using foreign exchange reserves, interest rates and the budget as policy instruments. *An Introduction to National Income Models* (Beecon) permits the user to construct and explore macro models by suggesting values for the model's parameters. *Introduction to Keynesian Economics* (Tutor Software) comprises a 45-page student text plus three disks and tutors' notes. Two of the disks contain self-assessment questions and five simulations; the third is a utilities program, for record-keeping and statistical operations. *Iron and Steel Location* (Longman) (for 14–16-year-olds) presents four historical episodes in which the costs of transporting coal and iron ore vary. Students are led to see how changes in such variables affect the location decision.

Fiscal Policy (Longman) would serve as a good 'warm-up' exercise for *Running the British Economy*. Its plausible underlying model links changes in demand and output to key target variables like the balance of payments, unemployment and inflation. Students act the role of 'Treasury economist', and control the economy by manipulating the levels of government expenditure and taxation, using one of four scenarios for the economy: booming, static, in recession or minus North Sea oil. The object is to keep national income near productive potential without causing severe inflation or balance of payments crises. *Gains from Trade* (Longman) uses examples where the benefits of international specialization are unequivocal. The program is intellectually challenging, and students will be compelled to think clearly about the problems of exchange rates.

The next development in CAL for economics and business education is likely to be material orientated towards 1992 and the Single European Market. An Association of European Economics Education Computer Working Group is establishing joint projects with a European dimension, the first of which have been mentioned above (*SECOS/EURECO*). An Economics Association group is currently collating a comprehensive listing of CAL programs, describing each program's value and limitations: a long-needed reference work. It is also producing a booklet providing classroom examples of the use of CAL in economics and business education.

Addresses

AVP Computing, Com 5/6, Hocker Hill House, Chepstow, Gwent.
Banking Information Service, 10, Lombard St, London EC3V 9AT.
Beecon, 16, Kingrove Ave., Nottingham NG9 4DQ.
BP Educational Service, PO Box 5, Wetherby, West Yorks LS23 7EM.
Longman Logotron, Dales Brewery, Gwydir St, Cambridge CB1 2LJ.
McGraw Hill, Shoppenhangers Rd, Maidenhead, Berks SL6 2QL.
Pitmansoft, 12/14 Slaidburn Cresc., Southport PR9 9YF.
RBRC Software, The Guild House, 32, Worple Rd, London SW19 4EF.
Software Production Associates, PO Box 59, Leamington Spa.

Statistics for Education, 13, Dennington Rd, Wellingborough, Northants NN8 2RL.
Tutor Software, Grove Lane, Wishaw, Sutton Coldfield, West Midlands.

References

Hurd, S. (1990) *EURECO*. Economics of Europe Database Vol. 1 General Economic Statistics (Statistics for Education).

18 Economics Textbooks at A and GCSE Level

David Whitehead

A Level Economics textbooks: a select list

Author	Title	Publisher	Date of latest edition
Anderton, A G	*Economics*	Causeway	1991
Anderson, A G	*Economics: A New Approach*	Unwin Hyman	1989
Atkinson, G B J	*Economics: Themes and Perspectives*	Causeway	1989
Beardshaw, J	*Economics: A Student's Guide*	Pitman	1989
Begg, D *et al.* Lipsey, R G and	*Economics*	McGraw Hill	1987
Harbury, C D	*First Principles of Economics*	Weidenfeld	1988
Livesey, F Maunder, W P J	*A Textbook of Economics*	Longman	1989
et al.	*Economics Explained*	Collins	1991
Paisley, R and Quillfeldt, J	*Economics Investigated*	Collins	1989
Perry, A	*Approaching Economics*	Stanley Thornes	1988
Stanlake, G F	*Introductory Economics*	Longman	1989
Stanlake, G F	*Macroeconomics*	Longman	1989

GCSE Economics: textbooks, revision guides and ancillary books for students and teachers

Textbooks

A Anderton, *Economics for GCSE*, Collins.
Bestseller!

M. Brimble, *Economics Explored*, Stanley Thornes.
Active learning approach, coherently integrated by an experienced teacher.

Theory is induced from the activities. Espouses a multicultural, gender-neutral stance. Lightly humorous, and highly suitable for mixed ability classes.

P Curry, *Economics: A Comprehensive Approach for GCSE*, Bell and Hyman.
Large visual element plus long sections of continuous text (Anderton has 87 units, Leake 56 chapters, Vosper 29 chapters, Curry 16 chapters). Strong coverage of Third World and ethnic minorities. High reading level required. Only a few, conventional questions. Rather heavy for GCSE. Worth having a desk copy for teacher.

S Hanan and G Hale, *Economics in Focus*, Hodder and Stoughton.
Geoff Hale is an ex-GCSE Chief Examiner, so the level of treatment is authoritative. But rather a brief text (127pp). Replete with jolly graphics, and some suggested coursework assignments. Adequate index.

A Leake, *Action Economics*, Macmillan.
More emphasis on text than Anderton. Plenty of case studies, but relatively few classroom tasks.

K B Marder and L P Alderson, *Economic Society*, 3rd ed, Oxford University Press.
Glossy 3rd edition, 'thoroughly revised to make it suitable for GCSE', a rather misleading comment. Few additions, for example, on privatisation. Updated data and layout, plus more data response and multiple choice questions.

D Moynihan and B Titley, *Economics: A Complete Course*, Oxford University Press.
442-page blockbuster, with as much graphics as text: very visually appealing. Excellent index. Accompanied by question and revision book (see below).

R Paisley and J Quillfeldt, *GCSE Economics*, Longman.
Caters for whole ability range. Densely written text, but clear and unpatronising. Clear tasks set. Good, workable coursework suggestions.

G F Stanlake, *Starting Economics*, Longman.
Comprehensive. Suitable for above average students. Main points summarized at chapter ends. Well thought out visuals. An adapted O-level text, with fewer activities than 'written-for-GCSE' texts.

G Teager, *Discover Economics*, Pitman.
Not a complete textbook but plenty of interesting case studies and ideas for work.

A Tibbitt, *Examining Economics*, Nelson.
Geared to active learning. Many visual features. Emphasis on activities rather than lengthy text. Wealth of data. Thorough coverage of typical syllabus. Careful use of language and very good index. Workable text appropriate for GCSE objectives.

C Vosper, *Money-Go-Round*, Blackwell.
Extensive text, plus versatile cartoon style, which integrates pictures, verbal comments and structured diagrams. Varied questions, but little emphasis on investigative approach, except through data response questions.

Revision guides

B Harrison, *GCSE Economics*, Longman Revision Guide.
Weighty content, with clear explanations, and up-to-date data. Extensive specimen answers and student answers with examiners' marks appended. Few student activities relieve long pages of text.

I C Hobday, *GCSE Economics*, Pan Study Aids.
Old-fashioned crammer.

K West, *Economics GCSE*, Letts Study Aids.
Revised O-level guide, with new units on data response and coursework, also summaries. Compares all Boards' syllabuses.

R Young, *Work Out Economics GCSE*, Macmillan Work Out Series.
A revision text, with topic summaries followed by various types of worked question. Strongly recommended.

D Moynihan and B Titley, *A Complete Course: Question and Revision Book*, Oxford University Press.
Provides coursework suggestions, as well as practice in multiple choice and short answer questions, structured essays and data response questions.

Ancillary student texts

J Bardsley and J Nettleship, *Economics Coursework Pack*, Causeway Press.
Covers micro and macro. 42 cards, copyright free. Mini-research projects based on hypotheses. Superb collection of lively, practicable ideas.

J. Bardsley and J Nettleship, *Coursework in Economics*, Causeway Press.
Advice for pupils on how to start research, data collection and presentation, and explanation of results plus 25 suggested topics. Strongly recommended for purchase as class sets.

D Fenn and R Pearce, *Data Response for GCSE Economics*, Blackwell.
Teachers may freely photocopy these 54 questions. Also a very useful 7-page introduction for teachers. Lots of photographs.

A Leake, *Countdown to GCSE*, Macmillan Education.
Intended for students and parents. Covers study skills needed, and gives advice on how to tackle examination questions and coursework. Compares all the syllabuses.

R Nutter, *Economics Understood*, Stanley Thornes.
A course companion of over 140 multiple choice and data response questions for GCSE.

D Sowden, *Living Economics*, Heinemann Educational.
Innovative approach. Very little text. Launches straight into tasks. Each double-spread takes a separate topic. Embraces spirit of GCSE. Not a course book, but useful as a stimulus, and as source of ideas. Suitable for less able students.

C Bancroft, *Assignments in Economics*, Nelson.
Covers main syllabus elements, with brief synopsis of material, data response and multiple choice questions, and suggestions for coursework assignments. 101 pages plus comprehensive 8-page glossary of economic terms: a useful mini economics dictionary for everyone.

Ancillary teacher texts

D Eastburn and R Gelder, *GCSE Coursework – A Teachers' Guide to Organisation and Assessment*, Macmillan Education.
For teachers: thorough advice. Radical approach via group work and student involvement in assessment procedure. Illustrates actual pieces of coursework, based for example on role play and field work. Reviews how to assess coursework, and explains criterion-referencing and the moderation process. Analysis is educationally provocative and of great practical value.

Economics Association, *Economics on Course*, Stanley Thornes.
Sections on different aspects of coursework, written by chief examiners and teachers. Student coursework activities included. Photocopiable in its entirety.

19 Annotated List of Useful Addresses

David Whitehead

Advertising Association, Abford House, 15 Wilton Road, London SW1V 1NJ.
Has national speakers made up of people from all sides of the advertising business, willing to speak on most aspects and in most areas of the country. Free booklets. An information centre open from 10.30a.m. to 1p.m. and 2.00p.m. to 4.00p.m., Monday to Friday, to all bona fide enquirers. Publications list. List of suggested reading. Priced resource books entitled *Finding out about advertising*, and *Advertising in perspective*, (A-Level Economics) available from CRAC Publications, Hobsons Ltd., Bateman Street, Cambridge CB2 1LZ.

Advertising Standards Authority, 2–16 Torrington Place, London WC1E 7HN.
The British Code of Advertising Practice, British Code of Sales Promotion Practice, annual reports, case reports, and free leaflets. Six videos/films (available from Viscom Audio Library, Unit B11, Park Hall Road Trading Estate, Dulwich, London SE21 8EL) details in leaflet from ASA.

Advisory Unit for Microtechnology in Education, Endymion Road, Hatfield, Herts AL10 8AU.
Provides microcomputer software packages. Runs courses for economics teachers in the Chiltern region. Offers advice and possibly speakers, in the field of CAL in economics.

Anforme Business Publications Ltd., 4 Duke's Court, Princess Way, Prudhoe, Northumberland NE42 6PL
Publishes *Business Studies* quarterly: contains articles and regular features particularly aimed at 'A' Level students.

Edward Arnold, Mill Road, Dunton Green, Sevenoaks, Kent TN13 2YA.
Catalogue of social science publications.

Associated British Ports, 150 Holborn, London EC1N 2LR.
Provides list of port addresses. School and student visits can sometimes be arranged at the discretion of the local port manager.

Associated Examining Board, Stag Hill House, Guildford, Surrey GU2 5XJ.
Produces booklet on examining Economics.

Association of Agriculture, Victoria Chambers, 16/20 Strutton Ground, London SW1P 2HP.
Specialist publications on all aspects of agriculture and the countryside, teachers' seminars and help with farm visits.

Association of British Insurers, Education Liaison Officer, Aldermary House, Queen Street, London, EC4N 1TT.
Resource list available upon request. Money Management Review – a termly publication available free to teachers and advisers; contact Education Liaison Officer for details. Address with effect from September 1991: 45–57 Gresham Street, London, EC2.

Association of European Economics Education. Secretary-General, Steve Hurd, Computers in Economics Unit, Staffordshire Polytechnic, Stoke-on-Trent, ST4 2DF.
Publishes journal, provides information about relevant national and international meetings, a regular information bulletin, helps to organise international contacts for teacher and pupil exchanges and international project work. £14 p.a. for individuals, £21 for institutional membership.

AVP, School Hill Centre, Chepstow, Gwent NP6 5PH.
Comprehensive guide to education software, plus individual subject catalogues of all education resources are available.

BAA plc, Corporate Communications, 130 Wilton Road, London SW1V 1LQ.
Information booklets, airport news, news releases, annual report, Heathrow facts and figures, information sheets on individual airports in UK.

Baltic Exchange, The Secretary, 14–20 St Mary Axe, London EC3A 9BU.
Booklet and factsheets describing the Baltic Exchange and its various markets. Visits to the Exchange are at 11.30a.m. and 12.30p.m. on weekdays (by appointment only, max 20 in a group).

Bank of England, Public Liaison Group, Threadneedle Street, London, EC2R 8AH.
Details may be obtained of the Bank of England Museum, including a list of presentations and film showings available to booked parties. A centralised booking facility is offered for 'City Insight', a trail of the City of London and its markets. Teachers' Resource Packs for Primary, GCSE and Advanced levels, containing teachers' notes, factsheets and wallcharts are available at a

cost of £14.50 (plus £1.50 postage and packing) directly from Hobsons Publishing PLC, Bateman Street, Cambridge CB2 1LZ. Available on free loan are copies of 'The Bank of England', on VHS video; a returnable deposit of £9.95, however, is required. *Bank Briefing*, a digest of the Quarterly Bulletin, is issued free of charge, a maximum of ten copies per school can be provided. Free factsheets on the workings of the Bank are also available.

Banking Information Service, 10 Lombard Street, London EC3V 9AT.
Contact: Maureen Cork. BIS produces a diverse range of both paper-based and interactive resources for the secondary age range. 'Financial Planning and Management of Design and Technology Projects' is a multi-media package designed to meet the needs of the Technology National Curriculum. 'City Link', economic software for Sixth Form students, aims to promote understanding of the City market places. Other materials, such as 'The Single Market – About Community Currencies', are designed to contribute to economic and industrial understanding across the curriculum. Write for a free colour catalogue.

Barclays Bank plc, 54, Lombard St., London EC3P 3AH
Publishes quarterly bank review.

BBC Education Information, Villiers House, The Broadway, London, W5 2PA.
Details of all BBC educational broadcasts and accompanying resources.

BBC Training Videos, Woodlands, 80 Wood Lane, London, W12 0TT.
Videos available for purchase on a wide range of business information and management training topics. Catalogue for all titles from above address.

Bell and Hyman Ltd., Denmark House, 37/39 Queen Elizabeth St., London SE1 2QB.

Blackwell (Basil), 108 Cowley Rd., Oxford OX4 1JF.

BP Educational Service, P.O. Box 30, Blacknest Road, Blacknest, Alton, Hampshire, GU34 4PX.
Catalogue of resources for schools and colleges; film catalogue.

BP Film Library, 15 Beaconsfield Road, London NW10 2LE.
Catalogue of free-loan films and videotapes.

British Association for Commercial & Industrial Education, 16 Park Crescent, London W1N 4AP.
Services include programmes of public and in-house courses specialising in trainer training; consultancy in training strategy and managing change; an Information Service on anything concerning vocational education and training; a journal; a specialist library and a Trainers' Bookshop.

British Coal, Schools Service, Public Relations Dept., Hobart House, Grosvenor Place, London SW1X 7AE.

Set of ten wall charts on Coal Today. Teachers' pack of booklets, leaflets and videos on coal and mining industry.

British Institute of Management, Africa House, 64/78 Kingsway, London WC2B 6BL.
BIM Books – a complete catalogue of publications.

British Insurance & Investment Brokers' Association, BIIBA House, 14 Bevis Marks, London, EC3A 7NT.
Represents 3,250 insurers brokers and independent financial advisers. Provides careers advice and youth training facility. Provides bursaries for students of insurance at universities and polytechnics.

British Invisible Exports Council, Windsor House, 39 King Street, London EC2V 8DQ.
Primary source for information on invisibles. Statistical cards, city guides and videos available.

British Telecom Education Services, British Telecom Centre, 81 Newgate Street, London EC1A 7AJ.
Publishes an education resources catalogue describing its full range of software programs, videos and publications.

Building Societies Association, 3 Savile Row, London W1X 1AF.
Teaching resources available covering money management, communication skills and housing.

Business & Technician Education Council (BTEC), Central House, Upper Woburn Place, London WC1H 0HH.
Approves vocational courses and awards qualifications at First, National and Higher National Certificate and Diploma level.

Butterworth-Heinemann Ltd, Westbury House, Bury Street, Guildford, Surrey GU2 5BH.
Catalogue of publications, *Industry & Higher Education* journal.

Cambridge Business Studies Project, 22 Nene Crescent, Oakham, Leics LE15 6SG.

Cambridge University Press, The Edinburgh Building, Shaftesbury Road, Cambridge CB2 2RU.

Careers Research and Advisory Centre (CRAC), 2nd Floor, Sheraton House, Castle Park, Cambridge CB3 0AX.
Runs courses and conferences for Economics and Business Studies teachers.

Causeway Press Ltd., PO Box 13, 48 Southport Rd., Ormskirk L39 5HF.

Centre for Alternative Technology, Machynlleth, Powys.
Demonstration centre on renewable energy, energy conservation and organic farming. Open daily from 10–5. Day and residential visits. Mail order infor-

mation service. Write to the Education Officer (with SAE) for further details.

Centre for Business Education and Education Management, Faculty of Education, Wolverhampton Polytechnic, Gorway, Walsall, WS1 3BD.
Courses are offered in Business and Enterprise Studies, Foreign Languages in Business and Education Management. These courses are available either as centre-based activities or outreach courses in LEAs' own venues. Also offers consultancy work with LEAs, TVEI projects and individual schools and colleges.

Centre for Industrial Studies, 1 Church Street, Grantham, Lincs NG31 6RR.
Centre seeks to support education/industry partnerships at regional and national level. Centre is base for a number of projects working to develop economic and industrial understanding. Runs training courses for teachers and industrialists, as well as working with teachers in classrooms. Centre also produces a number of publications concerned with supporting economic and industrial understanding.

Centre for World Development Education (CWDE), Regent's College, Inner Circle, Regent's Park, London NW1 4NS.
CWDE provides resources and advice on teaching about world development issues and north–south interdependence. Mail-order resources catalogue available listing over 400 items: books, leaflets, packs, computer software, audio-visual material and simulation games. Contact Education Officer for details.

Christian Aid, PO Box 100, London SE1 7RT.
Catalogue of publications and visual aids. Trading Game. Teacher/Sixth Form booklets: *Banking on the Poor*; *Real Aid: What Europe can do*; *Hungry Farmers – World Food Needs and Europe's Response*.

City of London, Public Relations Office, PO Box 270, Guildhall, London, EC2P 2EJ.
Publications about the City. A film lent on a pick-up/return basis to schools and colleges (a £20.00 deposit required). Conducted tours of Guildhall, Mansion House can be arranged, notification in writing necessary for Mansion House.

Collins Educational, Westerhill Rd., Bishop Briggs, Glasgow G64 2QT.

Committee of Advertising Practice, 2–16 Torrington Place, London, WC1E 7HN.
British Code of Advertising Practice, British Code of Sales Promotion Practice, case reports, free leaflets, free pre-publication copy advice, videos/films (available from Viscom Audio Library) details in leaflet from CAP. See also Advertising Standards Authority.

Commonwealth Development Corporation, 1 Bessborough Gardens, London SW1V 2JQ.
Information booklets, report and accounts, wall chart on its activities, film about Mananga Agricultural Centre.

Community Service Volunteers, 237 Pentonville Road, London N1 9NJ.
Volunteer programme and advisory service.

Concord Video and Film Council, 201 Felixstowe Road, Ipswich, IP3 9BJ.
Provides videos and films for hire and sale on domestic and international social issues including counselling, development education, the arts, race and gender issues, disabilities etc. for training and discussion. Video catalogue available.

Confederation of British Industry, Centre Point, 103 New Oxford Street, London WC1A 1BU.
Leaflet of current publications. Booklet about the CBI.

Conservation Trust, National Environment Education Centre, George Palmer Site, Northumberland Avenue, Reading RG2 7PW.
Aims to raise environmental awareness. Resource centre with loan facilities, information and speaker service, educational publications including study packs, topic cards, briefing notes. SAE for leaflet and publications list.

Conservative Research Department, 32 Smith Square, Westminster, London SW1P 3HH.
Publishes a campaign guide before each general election. Twenty pamphlets in the series *Politics Today* are published every year: some issues are on economic matters. Provides voluntary speakers upon request. The library, reference only, is open to *bona fide* students and researchers.

Consumer Credit Association of the UK, Queens House, Queens Road, Chester CH1 3BQ.
Trade association for the unsecured collected credit industry. Code of practice, information pack on consumer credit.

Consumers' Association, 2 Marylebone Road, London NW1 4DX.
Which? magazine monthly. Publications list.

Cooperative College, Education Department, Stanford Hall, Loughborough, Leciestershire LE12 5QR
Publishes information and learning materials including study manuals with practical exercises for use in schools and colleges. Groups may visit the Rochdale Pioneers Museum, Toad Lane, Rochdale.

Council for Education in World Citizenship, Seymour Mews House, Seymour Mews, London W1H 9PE.
CEWC helps to prepare British young people to take up their responsibilities

in an interdependent and multi-cultural world. It provides bi-monthly up-to-date objective information on topical issues (in versions for senior and junior students), a bi-monthly Newsletter (including new publications, events and other notices), a Speakers' Service (finding speakers for members), the administration of CO-Action (linking UK schools with UNESCO projects), support for conferences and other events on world citizenship themes, resources, advice and information.

Curriculum Centre for Teachers of Business Subjects, Studio 3A, Department of Education, Bristol Polytechnic, Redland Hill, Bristol BS6 6UZ.
Contact: David Drew. The Centre runs a wide range of INSET activities for teachers of Economics and Business Studies. Particular areas of interest include IT, flexible learning and schools/industry links.

Department of Education and Science, Elizabeth House, York Road, London SE1 7PH.
List of publications, including HMI paper on Economics and Business Education. Free from Room 3/77, DES.

East Midland Regional Examinations Board, Robins Wood House, Robins Wood Road, Aspley, Nottingham, NG8 3NR.
A member of the Midland Examining Group, offering a full range of GCSE examination syllabuses.

EcATT, Institute of Education University of London, 20 Bedford Way, London WC1H 0AL. Department of Education, University of Manchester, Oxford Road, Manchester M13 9PL.
EcATT is a partnership between industry and commerce, LEAs, central government and higher education. It aims to meet the long-term training needs of teachers, local authority coordinators, advisory teachers and others involved in the implementation of economic awareness programmes in schools and colleges. The major focus of work is individually tailored support and consultancy schemes for LEA teacher and curriculum development programmes in the 15–19 curriculum. These include specialist programmes in particular contexts (eg business education, pre-vocational, GCSE, links with industry, work experience and economic awareness in the primary school). Associate/Attachments on a full/part-time basis are available.

Economic and Industrial Awareness Programme, Manchester University, School of Education, Oxford Road, Manchester M13 9PL.
Support for institutions wishing to develop Economic and Industrial Awareness as a cross-curricular theme – support and training for co-ordinators, subject specialists, senior management and LEA/TVEI staff. EIAP serves a national network of over 20 LEAs.

Economics Association, 1a Keymer Rd., Hassocks, W. Sussex BN6 8AD

Publishes a quarterly journal, *Economics*; has a network of branches through-out the U.K., which organise meetings for teachers and students; publishes a large range of other books, articles and A–V resources; organises national conferences; represents Economics and Business Studies teachers on national bodies; runs curriculum development projects.

Economist Books Ltd., Axe & Bottle Court, Newcomen Street, London SE1 1YT.
Booklet cataloguing *The Economist* briefs and books.

Edge Hill College of Higher Education, Faculty of Initial Teacher Education, St. Helens Road, Ormskirk, Lancashire L39 4QP
Contact: Mr K Herbert (Economics) or Mr DI Gough (Business Education). The College, which is active in the education of teachers in the fields of Economics and Business Education, serves as the forum for a teachers' group, which normally meets once a term. College tutors also provide a consultancy service within the general field of economic understanding for colleagues in both primary and secondary schools. The College is particularly interested in the fields of Consumer Education and Economics and Business Education within a European context.

Educational Computing Unit, Cornwall House Annex, Waterloo Road, London SE1 8TX.
This Unit develops and evaluates educational software for Economics and Business Education for students from 13–20 years of age.

Employment Department, Public Enquiry Office, Caxton House, Tothill Street, London SW1H 9NF.
Students' guide on employment legislation, and list of publications. Applicants for booklets and speakers are considered on their individual merit.

Enterprise Education Unit, Durham University Business School, Mill Hill Lane, Durham DH1 3LB.
The unit produces enterprise education resource materials for teachers and pupils and runs a variety of training programmes for teachers in enterprise education; starter workshops for those relatively inexperienced in enterprise education; workshops to develop an enterprising style of teaching relating to the National Curriculum; workshops to develop techniques of managing the enterprise curriculum in schools; *Enterprise 14–16/16–19 An Educational Resource*. Obtained from the Enterprise Education Unit at Durham University Business School.

Equipment Leasing Association, 18 Upper Grosvenor Street, London W1X 9PB.
Booklets: equipment leasing, annual report.

Esmee Fairbairn Research Centre, Heriot-Watt University, Riccarton, Edinburgh, EH14 4AS.
Supplies economics programs for microcomputers.

Export Credits Guarantee Department, PO Box 272, Export House, 50 Ludgate Hill, London EC4M 7AY. ECGD Insurance Services, Crown Building, Cathays Park, Cardiff CF1 3NH.
Free leaflets are available detailing the services and activities of ECGD.

Finance Houses Association, 18 Upper Grosvenor Street, London W1X 9PB.
Booklets: 'A guide to credit and finance houses', 'Annual Report'.

Foundation for Education Business Partnerships, Suite 24, 10–18 Manor Gardens, London N7 6JY.
Local Education Business Partnerships are coming into existence to co-ordinate links between education and employers in a defined area (usually an LEA); economic and industrial understanding is one of their concerns. FEBP, launched in October 1990, is an independent national body whose tasks include supporting Partnerships. As part of this task, FEBP seeks to identify interesting practice and will also offer information services. FEBP is a useful source of information and advice on Partnership activity and on all aspects of collaboration between education and employers.

Framework Press Ltd, St Leonard's House, St Leonardgate, Lancaster LA1 1NN.
Framework offers study skills guidance for A-level Economics students, and photocopiable packs of student-centred activities in Business, Administration and Distribution for pre-vocational studies at 14+ (TVEI).

Friends of the Earth Trust Ltd., 26–28 Underwood Street, London N1 7JQ.
Information and educational sheets. Network of 300 local groups, some of which can provide speakers.

Further Education Unit, Grove House, 2–6 Orange Street, London WC2H 7WE.

General Agreement on Tariffs and Trade, Centre William Rappard, Rue de Lausanne 154, CH-1211 Geneva 21.
Booklets and leaflets relating to GATT. Annual reports on international trade and on GATT activities. Monthly newsletter *GATT Focus*. Accepts visits from student groups.

Girobank plc, Mrs A Hockey, Publishing & Design Branch, Bootle, Merseyside GIR 0AA.
Data pack gives comprehensive information on the history of Girobank, relationship with the Post Office, banking services offered to personal and business customers, operational procedures and computer equipment, with illustrations of transaction documents. Suitable for GCSE, CPVE, BTEC/SCOTVEC, Secondary, TVEI, YTS.

Greater London Enterprise, 63–67 Newington Causeway, London SE1 6BD.

A variety of corporate literature on GLE's development capital, industrial property, technology and training businesses.

Guild Education, 6 Royce Road, Peterborough PE1 5YB.
Wide selection of education curriculum videos including Open University – licensing and sales.

Heinemann Educational, Halley Court, Jordan Hill, Oxford OX2 8EJ.
Annual catalogue of business and economics books.

HMSO, Publicity Department, St. Crispins, Duke Street, Norwich, NR3 1PD.
Issues a range of leaflets, catalogues and listing of their publications.

Hobsons Press, Bateman Street, Cambridge CB2 1LZ.
Publishes The Bradford Game, part of the Production Programme.

Hodder & Stoughton Educational, Mill Road, Dunton Green, Sevenoaks, Kent TN13 2YA.
Catalogue of business studies books.

ICI (Imperial Chemical Industries plc), Schools Liaison Section, Group Personnel Department, PO Box 6, Shire Park, Bessemer Road, Welwyn Garden City, Herts AL7 1HD.
'Foundations of Wealth' video series. Catalogue and order form available from: ICI Videotape Library, 15 Beaconsfield Road, London NW10 2LE.

Independent Broadcasting Authority, 70 Brompton Road, London SW3 1EY.
The IBA Code of Advertising Standards and Practice. Leaflets on independent local radio and Channel 4 TV. Booklets on independent broadcasting and advertising control. On 1 January 1991 IBA was replaced by Independent Television Commission and the Radio Authority. Both based at Brompton Road until further notice.

INDTEL, Headway House, Ivy Road, Aldershot, Hants, GU12 4TX.
'Pathways to Partnership' a pack of modular material for use by tutors with students on courses of initial teacher education. Forty inter-related practical units relate to issues of economic, industrial and enterprise awareness. Sponsored by Guinness plc and available from INDTEL (Industry and Teacher Education Liaison).

The Industrial Society, Peter Runge House, 3 Carlton House Terrace, London SW1Y 5DG.

Inland Revenue Education Service, PO Box 10, Wetherby, West Yorks LS23 7EH.
A free brochure on resource material available.

Institute for Fiscal Studies, 180 Tottenham Court Road, London W1P 9LE.

List of publications. Free quarterly newsletter. Reduced membership rate for teachers.

Institute of Chartered Accountants in England and Wales, PO Box 433, Chartered Accountants' Hall, Moorgate Place, London EC2P 2BJ.
Careers booklets and careers video (available on free loan). Has network of local accountancy careers advisers for visiting schools and attending careers meetings or conventions. Contact Student Recruitment Section for further details.

Institute of Marketing, Moor Hall, Cookham, Berks SL6 9QH.

Intermediate Technology, Myson House, Railway Terrace, Rugby, CV21 3HT.
'Economics as if People Mattered' – the subtitle to *Small is Beautiful* by E.F. Schumacher, the founder of Intermediate Technology, gives an indication of IT's role in economics for a sustainable future – globally. IT's education office are producing material for the National Curriculum – particularly for Technology, with special regard to 'new' economic awareness as promoted by the New Economics Foundation. Income generation through small businesses is basic to the IT philosophy.

International Labour Office, Vincent House, Vincent Square, London SW1P 2NB.
List of publications; speakers can sometimes be provided.

International Monetary Fund, Publications Unit, Room C-100, 700 19th Street NW, Washington DC 20431, USA.
Publishes a catalogue of all books and periodicals that are currently available. Annual report is free of charge.

International Stock Exchange, Information & Promotions Department, London EC2N 1HP.
General leaflets are available explaining history and functions of the Exchange. Details of educational material available from the Education Liaison Officer.

John Lewis Partnership, Information Services, 171 Victoria Street, London SW1E 5NN.
Weekly house journal: *The Gazette*. Booklets about the organisation, reports and accounts, fact sheets concerning history, trading policies and democratic structure of the Partnership.

John Murray, 50 Albemarle Street, London W1X 4BD.
Catalogue of business and management studies books.

Labour Party, Information Unit, 150 Walworth Road, London SE17 1JT.
Materials on the Labour Party and its policies. Visits and talks at head office

should be arranged through the Information Unit.

Liberal Democrats, 4 Cowley Street, London SW1P 3NB.
Issues a number of leaflets on economic policy; programme for small businesses and the self-employed; profit-sharing and employee share ownership. Briefings on trade unions, fighting poverty, international development, rural regeneration. Speakers can be arranged. Visits to the party headquarters: a lecture is given about the party's policies and general principles, with ample time for questions.

Lloyds Bank plc, Economics Dept., 71, Lombard St., London EC3P 3BS.
Publishes monthly *Economic Bulletin*.

Lloyd's of London, Public Affairs Department, 1 Lime Street, London EC3M 7HA.
Booklets, 'Lloyd's Link' publication for schools. Video on Lloyd's. Visits to Exhibition and Viewing Gallery.

London Chamber of Commerce and Industry, Marlowe House, Station Road, Sidcup, Kent DA15 7BJ.
An examinations board offering National Vocational Qualifications and examinations in Business Studies, Languages and Secretarial Studies. Also publishes a quarterly journal, *Business Education International*.

London Discount Market Association, 39 Cornhill, London EC3V 3NU.
List of addresses of members of the Association.

Longman Group UK Ltd., Longman House, Burnt Mill, Harlow, Essex CM20 2JE.
Catalogue of publications.

Longman Logotron, Dales Brewery, Gwydir Street, Cambridge CB1 2LJ.
Longman Logotron is now the largest specialized provider of software to educational users in Britain. Software useful to teachers of Economics and Business Studies include: easy-to-use spreadsheets and word processors; business simulations and models; the renowned Heriot-Watt teaching model, Running the British Economy; and an electronic library of source documents. Catalogues are available on request.

Macmillan Education, Houndmills, Basingstoke, Hants RG21 2XS.

McGraw-Hill Book Company (UK) Ltd, Shoppenhangers Road, Maidenhead, Berks SL6 2QL.

Marks and Spencer plc, The Public Relations Department, Michael House, Baker Street, London W1A 1DN.
Student information packs suitable for GCSE and A level students.

Midland Card Services, 365 Chartwell Square, Southend-on-Sea, SS99 2UU.
Set of notes outlining the development of the Access and Visa credit card systems.

Midland Examining Group, The West Midlands Examinations Board, Norfolk House, Smallbrook, Queensway, Birmingham B5 4NJ.
The Group offers GCSE examinations in both Economics and Business studies.

National Curriculum Council (Information Section), Albion Wharf, 25 Skeldergate, York YO1 2XL.
The National Curriculum Council has an information section which offers advice on all aspects of the National Curriculum and on National Curriculum Council Publications. Technology, one of the ten foundation subjects of the National Curriculum, was introduced in schools from September 1990 and includes under its umbrella business education.

National Dairy Council, Education Department, 5–7 John Princes Street, London W1M 0AP.
The National Dairy Council's Business Studies Pack covers Technology generally for Key Stage 3 and specializes in Business Studies and Economic Concepts for Key Stage 4. It looks at the dairy industry from farming, through processing to sales and marketing. Wherever appropriate, cross-referencing is made to link with other subjects, attainment targets and programmes of study.

National Economic Development Office, Millbank Tower, Millbank, London SW1P 4QX.
Books include *NEDO in Print*, and *British Industrial Performance*. The Office is able to organize occasional visits by small Sixth-Form groups. These need to be planned well ahead and requests should be addressed to the Head of Communications section.

National Institute of Economic and Social Research, 2 Dean Trench Street, Smith Square, London SW1P 3HE.
Quarterly national economic review: £55 per annum. Leaflet of publications in print.

National Westminster Bank plc, Group Strategy and Communications, 41 Lothbury, London EC2P 2BP.
Economic reports on world and UK regions. The *Nat West Quarterly Review* and the annual report and accounts are available from: National Westminster Bank plc, Secretary's Office, 41 Lothbury, London EC2P 2BP.

Northcote House Publishers, Estover Road, Plymouth PL6 7PZ.
Publish a number of books in Economics and Business Studies and will be pleased to send a catalogue upon request.

Northern Ireland Schools Examinations and Assessment Council, Beechill House, 42 Beechill Road, Belfast BT8 4RS.

Office of Fair Trading, Room 305, Field House, 15–25 Bream's Buildings, London EC4A 1PR.
Pack of consumer publications.

Office of Population Censuses and Surveys, Census Information Unit, St. Catherine's House, 10 Kingsway, London WC2B 6JP.

Open University Educational Enterprises Ltd., 12 Cofferidge Close, Stony Stratford, Milton Keynes MK11 1BY.
Sells books, videos and audio cassettes originally prepared as Open University course materials.

Organisation for Economic Co-operation and Development, Publications Service, 2, rue Andre-Pascal, 75775 Paris, CEDEX 16, France.

Overseas Development Administration, Information Department, Eland House, Stag Place, London SW1E 5DH.
List of materials on overseas development and aid, bi-monthly newspaper *British Overseas Development*.

Oxfam, 274 Banbury Road, Oxford OX2 7DX.
Education catalogue, with addresses of regional offices and development education centres, and list of education materials for sale to teachers and students. Booklet of general and technical publications. List of free information sheets on Oxfam's work.

Oxford & Cambridge Schools Examining Board, Brook House, Purbeck House, Purbeck Road, Cambridge CB2 2PU.

Oxford University Press, Educational Division, Walton Street, Oxford OX2 6DP.
Publish annual catalogues in History, Economics and Business Studies.

Pictorial Charts Educational Trust, 27 Kirchen Road, London W13 0UD.
Leaflet of wall charts available.

Pitman Publishing, Periodicals Division, 128 Long Acre, London WC2 9AN.
Publishes *Business Education Today* monthly: it includes teaching materials, photocopiable assignments and reviews.

Philip Allen Publishers Ltd., Market Place, Deddington, Oxford OX5 4SE.
Publishes *Economic Review* five times p.a. Aimed at A level students.

Population Concern, 231 Tottenham Court Road, London W1P 9AE.
Leaflets and books including a yearly world population data sheet; advice on

films on population issues; speakers on population and related topics; list of publications.

Post Office Educational Resources, PO Box 145, Sittingbourne, Kent ME10 1NH.

Primary Schools and Industry Centre, Polytechnic of North London, Prince of Wales Road, London NW5 3LB, Director Dr. Alistair Ross.
Curriculum development and research relating to economic and industrial understanding in the primary school. Current projects include the Economic and Industrial Background Experience and Knowledge of Student Primary Teachers (funded by EATE) and Technology at Work (funded by Shell UK). Publications for sale include The Primary Enterprise Pack, Primary Schools and Industry Kit, Economic and Industrial Awareness in the Primary School, resource lists, case studies. A publications list is available from the Centre.

Project Trident, 91 Brick Lane, London, E1 6QN.
This industry and education backed organisation arranges work experience placements for 15- and 16-year-olds as part of a three-pronged programme which aims to give young people a better start in life. With over 70 projects nationally, it arranges for the secondment of managers from industry to provide a single point of contact between local employers and schools. It offers teachers extensive experience in the administration of work experience schemes; personal contact with employers resulting in a broad range of quality placements in both industry and the arts; a comprehensive analysis of the merits of each placement. A list of all Project Trident offices is available.

Routledge, 11 New Fetter Lane, London EC4AP 4EE.
Catalogue of books published.

Royal Economic Society, University of York, Heslington, York YO1 5DD.
Publishes the *Economic Journal.*

Royal Society of Arts Examinations Board, Westwood Way, Coventry, CV4 8HS.

SAGSET (Society for the Advancement of Games and Simulations in Education and Training, c/o Centre for Extension Studies, University of Technology, Loughborough, Leics LE11 3TU.
A professional society which aims to encourage the development of interactive learning through the use of simulations and games. Annual conference, journal (*Simulation/Games for Learning*) and resource lists of materials in a range of subjects.

Scottish Consultative Council on the Curriculum, Gardyne Road, Broughty Ferry, Dundee, DD5 1NY.
SCCC Information File, produced twice yearly, contains newsletters and details of publications.

Shell Film Library, Unit 2, Cornwall Works, Cornwall Avenue, Finchley, London NW4 4AT.
Catalogue of films and videos.

Shell Education Service, Shell UK Ltd., Shell-Mex House, Strand, London WC2R 0DX.
Catalogue of resources for teachers (free).

Society of Motor Manufacturers and Traders Limited, Forbes House, Halkin Street, London, SW1X 7DS.
For facts and figures and classroom materials about the UK motor industry and overseas, please contact Christopher Ford, Marketing and Publications Manager.

Stanley Thornes, Old Station Drive, Leckhampton, Cheltenham, GL53 0DN.

Sussex Publications Ltd., Microworld House, 2–6 Foscote Mews, London W9 2HH.
Sussex Tapes and Sussex Software. Audio cassettes on economics subjects.

Tesco Stores Ltd, Public Affairs Department, Tesco House, PO Box 18, Delamare Road, Cheshunt, Herts EN8 9SL.
Annual report, booklet on 'Help for The High Street', Tesco School Leaving Training Scheme leaflet, Linking with Education paper, employment initiatives.

The Panel on Takeovers and Mergers, PO Box 226, The Stock Exchange Building, London EC2P 2JX.
Annual Report of the Panel and Guide to the Panel.

Thomas Nelson and Sons Ltd., Nelson House, Mayfield Rd., Walton-on-Thames, KT12 5PL.

Trades Union Congress, Congress House, Great Russell Street, London WC1 3LS.
Video resource pack 'Why Trade Unions?', TUC guidelines on work experience for schoolchildren. *Learning about Trade Unions*: a book of activities and case studies aimed at teachers. Reading material on trade unions. List of TUC publications. Background notes and statistical information for teachers on trade unions. Booklets on trade-union issues such as health and safety, jobs, racism, equal opportunities, the health service, the social wage. Two-monthly *TUC Bulletin*, booklets 'Why Join a Union?' and 'Introducing the TUC'.

Treasury, Treasury Chambers, Parliament Street, London SW1P 3AG.
Publishes *Economic Briefing*, three times p.a. available free in bulk to educational establishments.

TVEI Unit (Teacher Support Section), The Training Agency, Employment Department Group, Sheffield S1 4PQ.

Supports Economics and Business Education in line with TVEI learning approaches and National Curricula. Has set up six Business Education Centres – Bristol, Wolverhampton, Sunderland, Canterbury, Aberdeen, Huddersfield – which develop new INSET and ITT. Other projects include developing teaching materials and courses in economic understanding and Enterprise Education. Mutual support provided through the TVEI National Business Education Teacher Development Network (NBETDN). Handbook available (currently free) researched by Sussex University for TVEI, to help heads and curriculum managers work out a whole-school policy for managing and delivering Business Education. Includes 16 case-studies and a supplement detailing NBETDN services for schools and (L)EAs.

Understanding British Industry, Information Centre, Sun Alliance House, New Inn Hall Street, Oxford OX1 2QE.
Information about UBI programmes including secondments for business and education and management education with an industrial perspective for senior educationists.

Unilever Education Liaison, PO Box 10, Wetherby, Yorkshire LS23 7EL.
Resources available include a series of booklets on Business Studies, UNISIM, a computer-based simulation, STANCE, a new role-play business exercise and the Foundations of Wealth two-part video. A free catalogue describing these resources and other general information on Unilever's activities is available by writing to Unilever.

United Kingdom Atomic Energy Authority, Education Service, B.354 West, Harwell Laboratory, Oxfordshire OX11 0RA.
Resources for teachers catalogue containing information on computer software, resources packs, videos, books, free publications, wall posters, Geiger counter, talks service, visits, *Atom* magazine, and teachers' seminars.

United Nations Information Centre, Ship House, 20 Buckingham Gate, London SW1E 6LB.
Many publications. Reference library. Audio-visual aids available on loan.

University of Cambridge Local Examinations Syndicate, Syndicate Buildings, 1 Hills Road, Cambridge CB1 2EU.
Reports on examinations, including analyses of multiple-choice tests. Meetings are arranged with schools both nationally and regionally.

University of London School Examinations Board, Stewart House, 32 Russell Square, London WC1B 5DN.
Syllabuses, reading lists, past papers and subject reports for A/AS examinations. INSET by arrangement with the Board.

University of Oxford Delegacy of Local Examinations, Ewert Place, Summertown, Oxford OX2 7BZ.
Supplies book lists, past papers and numerical answers, syllabuses, examiners'

ANNOTATED LIST OF USEFUL ADDRESSES **187**

reports, booklets on the examinations. Will provide speakers to groups of teachers, or visit schools, LEAs or teachers' centres.

Unwin Hyman Limited, 15-17 Broadwick Street, London W1V 1FP.
Catalogue of publications.

Urban Studies Centre, Harrow Club, 189 Freston Road, London W10 6TH.
USC offers a resource in terms of staff, information and facilities to schools and colleges. An excellent collection of historical and contemporary maps, plans, photographs, slides, published material and data concentrates on the Notting Dale area. Groups of students have combined field work, follow-up work on the resources and interviews with local contacts to examine economic aspects of the area in unusual detail.

Viscom Audio-Visual Library, Unit B11, Park Hall Road Trading Estate, London SE21 8EL.

Weidenfeld and Nicolson Ltd., 91 Clapham High St., London SW4 7TA.

Welsh Office, Economic and Statistical Services Division, Cathays Park, Cardiff CF1 3NQ.
List of publications. Booklet on government statistics: *A Brief Guide to Sources*. Films available from Central Film Library, PO Box 35, Wetherby, Yorkshire LS23 7EX.

World Bank, New Zealand House, London SW1Y 4TE.
Catalogue of publications; can provide occasional speakers.

World Development Movement, Bedford Chambers, Covent Garden, London WC2E 8HA.
Cross-party Third World pressure group. Publication list. Annual report. Currently working on sustainable development world bank policy, EC and the Third World.

Young Enterprise, Ewert Place, Summertown, Oxford OX2 7BZ.
Provides the opportunity for young people aged 15-19 years to experience the setting up through to liquidation of a company. Resource is in the form of a business kit and industrial advisers are provided as an integral part of the package. In addition, 'Into Business', an economic awareness package is available for 13-16-year-olds, within the curriculum.

Index